Practical ways to teach WRITING

L. I. N. C.
Dr. V. Johnston
West Kent Professional Development Centre
Tel. No. 0892 21872

Practical ways to teach WRITING

Editor: Bridie Raban

Contributors: Helen Arnold
 Anne Baker
 John Barrett
 Viv Edwards
 Irene Farmer
 Christopher Jarman
 Margaret Peters
 Bridie Raban

 Ward Lock Educational

First published 1985 by
Ward Lock Educational
47 Marylebone Lane
London W1M 6AX

A member of the Ling Kee Group
Hong Kong · Taipei · Singapore · London · New York

© Ward Lock Educational Co. Ltd 1985
Chapter 1 © Bridie Raban 1985
Chapter 2 © Anne Baker 1985
Chapter 3 © John Barrett 1985
Chapter 4 © Helen Arnold 1985
Chapter 5 © Irene Farmer 1985
Chapter 6 © Viv Edwards 1985
Chapter 7 © Margaret Peters 1985
Chapter 8 © Christopher Jarman 1985

All rights reserved. No part of this publication may
be reproduced, stored in a retrieval system, or
transmitted, in any form or by any means, electronic,
mechanical, photocopying, recording or otherwise,
without the prior permission of Ward Lock
Educational Co. Ltd.

British Library Cataloguing in Publication Data
Practical ways to teach writing. —(WLE primary
   handbooks)
   1. Language arts (Elementary)
   I. Raban, Bridie
   372.6'23   LB1575.8

ISBN 0-7062-4569-5

Design by Hickey Press Limited
Printed by William Clowes, Suffolk

Contents

Contributors   9

Foreword   11

1   Writing: an introduction   13
     by Bridie Raban

2   Real writing, real writers:
     a question of choice   15
     by Anne Baker

3   Writing from first-hand experience   20
     by John Barrett

4   The dilemma of creative writing   25
     by Helen Arnold

5   Organising writing together   33
     by Irene Farmer

6   Beyond Babel: linguistic diversity and
     children's writing   48
     by Viv Edwards

7   Purposeful writing   55
     by Margaret Peters

8   The neglected 'R'   71
     by Christopher Jarman

Index   79

True ease in writing comes from art, not chance
As those move easiest who have learned to dance.
An Essay on Criticism
Alexander Pope (1688–1744)

Contributors

Helen Arnold was, until recently, County English Adviser for Suffolk County Council. She is now teaching part-time at Homerton College, Cambridge, and lecturing and writing on aspects of language and education. She was research associate on the Schools Council's 'Extending Beginning Reading' project, and has since published books on aspects of reading. Her admiration of children's writing is long-standing, and she edited two county anthologies of Suffolk children's writing while adviser there.

Anne Baker has taught for eighteen years in primary and secondary schools and currently teaches juniors at Courthouse Green Primary School, in Coventry. She is Secretary of the NATE Primary Committee, a member of NATE's Language and Gender Working Party and is a teacher member of the CNAA Language and Literacy Panel. She reviews for *The School Librarian*, has written for *English in Education* and made a major contribution to *Children Reading to their Teachers* (NATE, 1984).

John Barrett has been teaching for eighteen years in schools that have served rural, urban and development areas. He has experience in primary and junior schools, both as a class teacher and head teacher and is currently Primary Adviser for West Sussex. He is especially concerned with the development of a curriculum based on the reality of the child's experience and is a regular contributor to in-service courses on this theme.

Viv Edwards decided to train as a teacher after finishing a Ph.D. in linguistics. Having identified language in education as her main research interest, she did not want to work alongside teachers without a full understanding of what was involved in their work. The experience was suitably humbling! She is currently Lecturer in Applied Linguistics at Birkbeck College, University of London, and regularly contributes to the initial and in-service training of teachers at Bulmershe College of Higher Education and the University of Reading. Her writing includes *The West Indian Language Issue in British Schools* (Routledge & Kegan Paul, 1979) and *Language in Multicultural Classrooms* (Batsford, 1983).

Irene Farmer is a Senior Lecturer at Bretton Hall College of Higher Education, Wakefield. For the past five years, half her college timetable has been spent working in schools with children and teachers as part of the Bretton Language Development Unit's programme. With her LDU colleagues, Angela Wilson and John Dixon (consultant), she has published a series of booklets on children's writing in the middle years. Her teacher training and early teaching experience was in primary schools, followed by a joint honours degree in psychology and sociology, a year in the Schools Council's 'Middle Years of Schooling' project, and three years of full-time research in infant schools for her Ph.D. on aspects of children's language development.

Christopher Jarman is In-service Coordinator at the Roehampton Institute, London. He has taught in primary schools for over twenty years as class teacher and head teacher and was Primary Adviser in Oxfordshire. He has written many articles and books for primary teachers including the widely-used handwriting scheme *Handwriting Skills*. He is on the national council of NAPE (National Association for Primary Education) and was the first editor of the *NAPE Journal*.

Margaret Peters was Tutor in Literacy at the Cambridge Institute of Education. A Froebelean, turned psychologist, she taught in primary schools before becoming an educational psychologist and later a College of Education lecturer. Her concern has always been that children should be free to write, and her research and writing on spelling has been to this end. Her writing includes *Spelling: caught or taught?*, published by Routledge & Kegan Paul in 1967 (a completely new revision has now been published entitled *Spelling: caught or taught? A new look* (1985)), *Success in Spelling*, published by the Cambridge Institute of Education in 1970 (the publication of her Ph.D. thesis), and the *Diagnostic and Remedial Spelling Manual* (Macmillan, 1975).

Bridie Raban was a remedial teacher for thirteen years, working with primary and secondary pupils, as well as adults. More recently she has been engaged in research and lecturing in the field of language and education at the University of Reading. She has published articles in *Child Education*, *A Question of Reading* with Cliff Moon and *Guides to Assessment in Education – Reading* (both published by Macmillan).

Foreword

This book is a collection of papers written for teachers and student teachers by colleagues who have spent many years in primary classrooms. The theme of the book is practical, although the contributors' understanding of the writing development of young children is clearly revealed as the basis for their suggested classroom activities.

The skill of an author has long been perceived as essentially mysterious and while many people have completed schooling as competent handwriters, few have ever glimpsed the possibilities revealed through the experience of real writing. An experience with a powerful force to shape thought and generate new worlds. Without this experience it is difficult, if not impossible, to initiate a young child into the process of becoming a writer.

More recently, our understanding of this process has increased and we are becoming more confident in acknowledging the appropriate experiences we wish to share with young children. This book addresses itself to those experiences, ways of thinking about them and ways of sharing them with the children in our classrooms.

Bridie Raban
July 1984

Writing: an introduction
Bridie Raban

Great emphasis has been placed on the teaching of reading during the primary school years, with less attention being paid to the writing development of young children. Writing, when it has been considered, has frequently been couched in terms of handwriting alone, but has rarely included the conscious effort to shape and mould aspects of authorship in children from the beginning of their school experience.

Writing in infant classrooms, for instance, can become a repetitive daily chore involving drawing a picture and then dictating a caption to the teacher for later tracing or copying. Little care or attention is given to the generation of these pieces other than a request from the teacher to 'write a story' or 'do some writing'. Teachers, when asked, claim that they insist on some writing from their pupils each day. They do this in the belief that regular practice in 'doing some writing' will contribute to their children's writing development in the long term. In reality, this enforced ritual may well be as useless and stultifying as hearing all children read aloud each day. How much more usefully could all this time be spent.

Real writing in school demands a reorientation of the focus of attention for many teachers. Anne Baker, in the second chapter in this book, identifies this change in her own work with children. She stresses the need for children to be actively involved in their own writing and how opportunities to re-write give children the chance to re-think and thus discover meaning more powerfully. For this to happen in school, real writing needs purpose, opportunity and time. Time needs to be taken to decide that you have something you want to say, children must be left to make up their own mind to write something – she stresses that these key choices must be left with the children. Children need to be left free to choose when to write and for how long.

The professional change which is required to ensure this possibility is one from teacher-focused writing demands towards child-orientated opportunities for writing, a change which sees children at the centre of their own lives. Once this shift in perspective is allowed to happen, the teacher's role moves towards one of suggesting, encouraging, discussing and facilitating the children in what they want to do in writing. Anne Baker writes about the nature of this change in her professional career and gives examples of her own classroom practice and the children's writing which this fosters.

John Barrett sees the task of the teacher as one of helping children understand themselves and their world. He stresses the educating force of writing in the daily lives of young children and illustrates how he uses writing as part of the everyday life of the classroom. He shows how all the everyday things that happen to children constitute their own world, and how these first-hand experiences can be captured and reflected upon through the activity of writing. Writing slows up the process of incidental experience and heightens it, giving time for a response to develop and for children to reflect on their world.

With personal experience, which is valued, comes authority and confidence in the world of everyday life – an ambition we would all have for our children. Development in writing, he claims, comes from a growing need to articulate this personal experience. However, in order for this to happen, these experiences must be valued and trusted by both the children and their teachers. John Barrett discusses what this looks like in a busy classroom and through examples of children's writing he illustrates the value to teachers and children which such an approach can create.

Personal writing, from both first-hand experience and imagination, for children and adults, is intellectual and emotional. Helen Arnold poses the question 'How should we, as teachers, respond to this?'. She points out the need to help young writers to appreciate what they have done in writing. Young children, like all writers, not only select from experience in the retelling of events, but inevitably distort the facts to fit an artistic or psychological purpose. In responding to this writing we must, therefore, look at it as a whole.

We must be particularly aware, Helen Arnold stresses, of the way in which the selection and focusing of events has, or has not, conveyed an essence, or truth, which goes beyond the original experience. What we are looking for in writing is a total response, one which includes elements of intellect and emotion. Again she points out how development in children's writing is through finding a real purpose and she discusses ways of making this possible in classrooms.

Children need to find their own voice in their writing. This will be evident to them while composing, if they are encouraged to listen for their voice reverberating in their head while they write. These reverberations will assist the associative linking which is unique to each writer, and teachers can talk about these images and their juxtaposition with children, as they appear in their work. Teachers cannot teach creativity, they need to find ways of drawing on elements already in the children's minds and they will need to build features of open-endedness into the curriculum. Helen Arnold makes it clear that evaluation of such writing should be a shared enterprise and that if it is worth doing, it is worth doing together.

Organisation in writing is both at the level of the context in which writing takes place and within the writing itself. Irene Farmer points out how an awareness of the underlying structures in children's writing will help teachers in a number of different ways. Structure in writing displays thinking and through this teachers can be aware of the achievement in thinking which is taking place for children, they can be aware of the demands of different types of writing, and intervene helpfully as they work with children to shape their own thinking. She also considers some useful starting points for writing and suggests alternatives to copying from books by helping children with note-taking and the organisation of information from a wide range of sources.

What of children who speak English as a second language or speak a non-standard form? Viv Edwards shows how our work with these children is no different from our work with those children who speak standard English. In terms of their writing development, their needs are similar. She shows how linguistic diversity need not be seen as a problem, but rather as a resource. The felt need on the part of the teacher to eradicate differences can give way to a desire to capitalise on children's first language and engage them in dialogue in writing. Indeed, if the teacher can generate written responses to children's writing, then her writing provides stimulating models of standard written form for the children to absorb.

This idea of dialogue in writing is a familiar notion and reference to it can be found in the work of Laurence Sterne (1713–68). In *Tristram Shandy* he makes the point: 'Writing, when properly managed, ... is but a different name for conversation.' (*Tristram Shandy*, Penguin 1970, Oxford University Press 1983). Margaret Peters sees dialogue, or conversation, in writing at the base of purposeful writing, writing that is urgent and demands action. We write because we feel strongly about something, we write because we must. This reinforces the point of view already stated by others that stimuli from outside the child are capable of denying the need to write, which must come from within. When writing comes from within the child, Margaret Peters points out, both spelling and handwriting take on an appropriate importance.

It is clear that highly motivated activities demand precision, and if a response is required to a piece of writing then children will make sure that the writing is readable. Such writing happens frequently at home for young children, but how can we foster such 'urgent' writing in school? Margaret Peters illustrates what she means by 'silent conversations' using examples from written dialogues which have taken place in classrooms.

Writing of any kind would be impossible without the skill of handwriting and Christopher Jarman reminds us all of the need to attend to this aspect of authorship from the very beginning. Not that this aspect of the activity should take precedence over the urgency of composition, but that the correct formation of the letters of the English alphabet system should not be left to chance. Through art work, the natural patterns of children's scribbles and movements can be selectively reinforced towards the unnatural discipline of the alphabet. Christopher Jarman makes it clear that copying alone, without discussion, is a useless aid towards correct letter formation. This discussion and sharing is a part of the process of writing which needs as much guidance and support as the other aspects of authorship.

All the contributors to this book place the emphasis on learning to write with the children. It is they who must decide what to write, when and for how long. The task of the teacher is to ensure that there are experiences in school which demand a written response and that they, in their turn, respond to the children's writing. Most importantly, teachers must learn to respond to the messages which children send in writing, the meaning of their written statements, and work with children towards the refinement of their craft. Teachers who write alongside their children will become more aware of the pitfalls and the pleasures of capturing real and imagined worlds in writing.

Reference

Stern, L., *Tristram Shandy*, Penguin 1970, Oxford University Press 1983.

Real writing, real writers: a question of choice
Anne Baker

'We have nothing to rely upon in making our choices but ourselves.' (Richards, 1929)

Writing and reading are part of everyday reality in our society. They are ways in which we relate, share our thoughts and feelings, live and learn. I am writing, now, because I have something to say; you are reading, now, to find out my meaning. If we couldn't write, or read, we would be social cripples.

Writing I meet requires me to feel, to think, to act, to reflect, to refer, to know, to notice. It appears in the shape of bills, forms, statements, signs, advertisements, newspapers, magazines, reference books, novels and so on. It actually makes a difference to how I live my life. I respond to a political census, a tax return and an application form by filling them in; I believe that what a newspaper tells me *is* the news; I have been persuaded by an advertisement into buying a certain product; I have had confirmation of what I know in a piece of information; I have been moved by a narrative. Whether I read a little, or a lot, my life is influenced by writing.

As a reader, it seems to me that writers have a certain power. This power lies most obviously in their ability to communicate their purposes to me, perhaps to change me. As a writer, I feel that the possible power I have to change other people is significantly less important than the power which comes from actual involvement in writing. I write, and therefore I have a way of thinking and feeling, and a way of looking at and finding out about life, which amounts to a way of living.

I am involved in writing, now, to search for and discover what I mean and believe to be true about writing. My thoughts emerge, slowly, onto paper, and then I ponder them to decide if I've said what I really intend. I think my written thoughts over, go away and come back, if necessary, and they are still there, holding my meaning steady. If I want, I can rewrite my thoughts, which is to rethink them, and so, gradually, through writing, discover my meaning, what the truth is, for me. I live through, and let go of, my thoughts and feelings as I write; I get to know myself a bit better, I learn and I change.

The whole point of being a writer, it seems to me, is that you change as you write, you change yourself, you change the way you think. (Lessing, 1980)

Real writing is purposeful communication by writers to their readers. Real writers are those involved in writing for the purpose of communicating their own thoughts and/or feelings to their readers, which may include themselves. When they write, real writers participate in a process which I understand to be a question of choices made by the writers themselves. The process for each writer, whatever their stage of development, is something to do with these decisions.

- Deciding you have something to say to yourself, to another person, or to some people.
- Making up your mind to write something.
- Deciding on the form your writing will take.
- Allotting the time you need to write.
- Discovering by writing just what it is you have to say.
- Getting what you have to say right before letting go of it.
- Choosing whether, or not, to publish what you have written, and where.
- Entrusting what you have written to your reader, or readers.

People usually learn to write at school when they are children, because as children they have to go to school and schools elect to teach writing. Schools have tremendous potential for being the right sort of places for real writing to happen. Each school is a miniature society with a life of its own, that is different from home and different from outside society, a kind of meeting place of the two, the private and the public. Each school is a local and therefore known community of children and adults, the individual and the group, in richly complex relationships. Just the sort of place where children can use writing very much as real writers do in society as a whole, to live with, to learn with, to relate, to share.

They will only do this, however, if the life of the school is right, if it is concerned with children's own learning, if it provides a context in which children can participate in the writing process. Such a context is one in which children are free to do their own writing, to make their own choices. When they decide they have something to write, they are given the time and opportunity to carry out their purpose, to explore what they think and feel through writing, and to find out what they mean, at their own pace. They can invent or discover for themselves the form which does most justice to their closest concern. They can publish it if they please. They can learn to trust their authentic voices and to entrust what they have written to the eyes of their readers. Such a context is one in which teachers assist children in their writing, rather than direct what they must do. They do this by emphasizing to children that the only reliable choices in writing are those which they make for themselves. This is the context for real writing, in which real writers best grow. This is the context in which children, from first freely making marks on paper, can develop as real writers along a continuum of real writing that could stretch throughout their lives. It is also the context in which teachers, by paying a real attention to what children do, can come to accept and respect children, as of right, for what they are, what they are interested in and what they have to say.

Unfortunately, in spite of the fact that schools place an enormous emphasis on writing – apparently sixty per cent of children's time is spent in writing in school – much of the school-writing I see isn't real. It isn't real because it isn't generated by the purpose of its writers, but rather by their teacher's. It isn't trying to do the things I know writing can do: change, persuade, move, influence, inform. It doesn't reflect the living nature of writing going on in our society, of which schools are, after all, a part. It isn't real, and, if the writing isn't real, then neither are the writers.

When I enquire what is happening in schools where the writing isn't real, I find that the context for writing is very different from the one I have described and the procedure used for getting writing opposite to the writing process as I understand it. Crucially, in schools where the writing is directed, children are not consulted as to whether they have anything to say, and, if and when they have, it is not considered to be of central importance. 'Deciding you have something to say' and 'making up your mind to write something' are key choices in the writing process, because on one, or the other, or both of them, rest all the other choices to be made. If children aren't allowed to make the key choices, but are forced to accept someone else's decisions as to what is going to be said and written, then the writing process is crippled and any other decision is not worth making. Interestingly enough, in schools where the writing isn't real, children aren't allowed to make any other choices, anyway. It is the teacher who makes most of the decisions about writing, the school organisation seeing to the rest, and it is the teacher and his/her teaching which are the focus of attention.

What are the differences between schools where there is an awareness of the way in which the process of writing involves the writer in making a series of choices and decisions, and those where the teacher makes all the decisions?

- Instead of children deciding they have something to say, the teacher decides what is going to be said by presenting a stimulus, a topic, a theme or an interest. The teacher sets an exercise or worksheet, or gives notes, or requires feedback on what he/she has taught. The teacher prepares an examination or a test. The teacher is then the only audience for whom the children write. He/she collects the 'work' and reads it.

- Instead of children making up their minds when to write something, the teacher decides that children will write in the writing lesson when they do write.

- Instead of children deciding on the form their writing will take, the teacher, either explicitly, by saying so, or implicitly, by directing children to exercises, dictates form. Thus there are thirty stories, thirty poems, thirty adverts, thirty letters, thirty essays. There are language laboratories, course books, source books, workbooks and worksheets.

- Instead of children allotting the time they need to write, it is the school timetable and other organisational constraints which determine when the writing lessons are, and children have to write in these lessons which start and end at pre-set times.

- Instead of children discovering just what it is they have to say, much of their writing is carried out in the form of exercises which the teacher decides upon. There is such a thing as 'writing practice'.

- Instead of children getting what they have to say right, through as many drafts as are needed, before letting go of it, stories, letters, poems and so on, are usually produced as 'one-offs', or else written once in 'rough' and then in 'neat'. They are then 'marked' and corrected as finished products, judged by the teacher as right or wrong, good or bad. Paper, and its use, is strictly limited.

- Instead of children choosing whether or not to publish what they have written, and where, the teacher chooses 'neat' copies of children's writing to put on the walls. Sometimes, any and all kinds of writing go on the walls. The teacher asks for writing to go into children's notebooks, which are then put away into desks or trays until the books are full. The books are then kept in cupboards, or on offer to be taken home, or placed in the bin.

- Instead of children entrusting what they have written to their reader or readers, the teacher reads children's writing and endorses it with ticks or crosses, and maybe makes a critical comment and adds a score. The teacher notices those children who cannot cope with the conditions set for writing, and perhaps describes them as 'slow-learners', or lazy, or lacking in concentration, and prescribes more of the same thing to remedy the situation. He/she perhaps praises those children who can cope with the conditions, and describes them as hard-working and 'bright', and uses their success to justify continuing to teach in the same way.

In schools where the writing isn't real, where the teacher or the school makes the decisions at every stage of the writing procedure, the children are expected merely to practise and perform. They are not involved in making choices for themselves, their purpose isn't their own, they are not real writers. It seems to me that in such schools the teacher spends too much time trying to teach writing to children, and not enough time helping them to write. To keep writing real, it must be used. More than that, a person's language can't be separated from them, the living person is in their language. So, to try to impose a language process, such as writing, from outside, as a thing to be taught, to be transmitted, is to misunderstand the nature of language, and of people.

In my present school, the priority is 'getting real writing going in real situations where a real commitment to meaning becomes possible' (Burgess *et al.*, 1973).

- The children choose when to write and for how long.
- Children who want to write for themselves do so, and their privacy is respected.
- Children with a story to tell narrate it and have it typed into their story book, if they wish, to be placed on the shelf and read along with commercially-produced books, or presented to the person for whom it was written.
- Children who want to communicate with people outside school write letters, post them and receive replies.
- Labels are written by children to accompany objects they have brought in to display.
- Experts at gardening, bird-watching, or dinosaurs, write what they know into books and folders and posters, for themselves, or as a resource for other children to use.
- Favourite books generate reviews recommending that they be read.
- Notices for clubs, their registers and planned activities appear.
- Experiments are set up with accompanying instructions for carrying them out.
- Notes are made, and compared, as observations are carried out on snails, worms, flowers, insects, or whatever the children find arouses their curiosity.

Here, Steven, aged nine, uses writing for a very personal reason, to come to terms with the death of two birds. He writes in his Nature Notebook, which he lets other children, and me, read:

> Today me and Paul buried the second bird that we found. And I feel responsible for the little fellow's life, but he isn't alive any more, so I can't feel responsible, but I do anyway. So there, to everybody who's there.

And again:

> And yesterday we found a dead bird, but we didn't get a look in when Mrs Minns said some of her class could bury that one. But I suppose I was just feeling responsible for it.

Finally, he writes to me in a book he uses to evaluate what he has done each week (and to which I reply):

> I loved doing the piece on the Swan and the dead birds. I think I have got rid of my responsibility for them.

Steven's confidence in his own written voice, here, is an example of what happens when children have 'a way of interpreting life for themselves and a tradition of writing for themselves that has more chance of surviving than an everlasting insistence on writing to a formula' (Rosen and Rosen, 1973).

On request, Elaine instructs how she made a pink, papier-mâché pig she has brought to school. With help from her older sister, she writes some notes which she transforms into a poster (see page 18). Her poster is then pinned up in the art area until everyone who wants to make a pig has done so.

An example of a different kind of writing, for a different purpose, is found in Jonathan's 'Horror Films' (page 19). Jonathan is fascinated by horror stories and films but also frightened of them at the same time. He writes a powerful description of his feelings which he shows to me and which we talk about. Later, he asks me to type up his work which he then illustrates in bloodthirsty fashion. Together we read his resulting book to the rest of his class. Many children respond spontaneously with stories about their own fantasies and fears and it is with some relief that Jonathan realises that the ambiguity of his feelings is recognised and shared by others.

Elaine's poster

It is hard to change from being a teacher who makes all the decisions about writing, to being one who lets the children choose. The professional change, for me, came with the beginnings of personal change. It involved seeing children as individuals at the centre of their own lives, as people with something to say, and capable of making up their minds to say it and with the right to do so. It involved removing myself from the focus of attention in writing (and, incidentally, in everything else). I still had ideas, but I stopped walking in with an idea for all and tried to let my ideas be responses to the children's needs. I encouraged the children to be their own resource, and to look to themselves and each other for inspiration and support, as well as to me. I got out from being their audience, unless they actively chose me, when I replied, and I helped children to think of other people they might have something to say to in writing. I started listening to them, trying to get behind their heads to see the way they were coming at what they were trying to say. I began to let them make up their own minds and value their own judgements, because, in the end, they have nothing to rely on in making their choices but themselves.

In his book, *Freedom To Learn*, Carl Rogers says, 'My experience has been that I cannot teach another person how to teach. To attempt it is for me, in the long run, futile.' As teachers, we can reflect, perhaps wryly, on his honesty, for none of us was taught how to teach. We know we learned to teach by teaching.

> **Horror films**
>
> I like horror films because they are scarey. And best of all is when there are blood stains from people who killed each other.
>
> And when my sister wants to go to the loo, she runs up stairs and she would run down the stairs. And I know why she does that: because she thinks there's something, like a ghost, following her up.
>
> And in Jaws' film I daren't watch the bit when these two men go out to sea and they find a boat. And one man goes diving and sees a tooth. I thought it was Jaws' tooth. And then he saw a man and he dropped the tooth and he got on the boat as quickly as he could. And when that part started I got a pillow over my face.
>
> We watch horror films any time. And best of all are skeletons with blood stains over them and all blood stains over the floor. And we have crisps to eat and cups of tea to drink, and I feel sick sometimes when I watch horror films that's scarey. But I feel happy when they go back to the shop. And the name of the shop is Fossett's.
>
> And I know why the film is scarey because there are skeletons and blood stains over the floor, and people kill the other people in the film. But I feel sad for them. But it's the film which needs to be done.

Jonathan's 'Horror Films'

Real writing, the sort that is part of everyday reality in our society, the sort that can help children to make discoveries about themselves and their relationships with other people, is like teaching. It cannot be taught either. Real writers learn to write by writing.

This paper was previously published in *English in Education* Vol. 15, No. 3, pp.1–5 (1981).

References

Burgess, C., *et al.*, *Understanding Children Writing*, Penguin Education, London, 1973.
Lessing, D., *Interview with Doris Lessing*, BBC 2, 1980.
Richards, I. A., *Practical Criticism*, Routledge, London, 1929.
Rogers, C., *Freedom To Learn*, Merrill, 1969.
Rosen, C. and H., *The Language of Primary School Children*, Penguin Education, London, 1973.

Writing from first-hand experience
John Barrett

At the heart of the teaching task lies the responsibility of helping children to understand themselves, the world they live in, and the possibilities that those two elements present. It is generally accepted that primary-age children learn most effectively through their activities. It is in the interaction between each child and what lies before them at that moment that children extend their knowledge of the world. It is writing that, in turn, provides one of the principal means of construing meaning from those interactions.

In practical terms these are the needs:

- To create a context that offers a diet of varied experiences that are perceived by each child to be interesting, relevant and purposeful, and that can properly accommodate the pace of those experiences and the consequent exploration and expression of them.
- To create a climate that is conducive to writing, hospitable to the children's growing control over the written word, and that demonstrates the value it attaches to written tasks in its treatment of them.
- For teachers to understand the nature of the process, to enable them to support the child in exploring and making sense of the experience; that is, making sense as it were, for the child. We can, after all, only make sense of the child's sense.
- For the sustained and shared effort of the whole staff to help children develop a taste for the written word and the will to extend their control over it.
- It requires, above all, a clear perception of what purpose the writing is playing.

Understanding their world

The following examples arise from the original objective of 'helping children understand themselves and their world'. It is the incidental moments, the close-at-hand artefacts and experiences that constitute 'their world'. The special occasion and the treat can always be exploited in one way or another, but they are not the prerequisite for purposeful writing. The school and its curriculum provide a temporary and artificial environment but it is one in which we can engineer the circumstances and the climate that will invite interest and lead to productive experiences. The first six examples are taken from the topic of one child. They are not included because they represent outstanding pieces of work; on the contrary, they are chosen simply to illustrate how writing, when arising from personal experience, has, in a low key way, its own special quality, as well as playing a significant educational role.

Zoe (eight years) begins her topic:

> I like gerbils they fascinate me. They are furry and warm and they are nice to hold. They are one of my favourite animals. I would love to buy one for a pet.

From the teacher's point of view what is evident is Zoe's genuine engagement with the gerbils. While the degree of 'fascination' has yet to be put to the test it provides a promising start to her topic. For Zoe, in the process of writing, in selecting and arranging her words, even in such a short piece, has perhaps come a little closer to understanding the nature of her response. She comments in her next piece:

> When I put my tube (cardboard roll) in the gerbil cage this is what they did. First they went in and out of it and then they chewed and chewed it. It was like an adventure.

She happily attributes the gerbils with her feeling of adventure. This is a common enough feature. It demonstrates her sense of identification with them and thereby her likely commitment to her topic, and, in turn, the degree to which her teacher might exploit her interest.

Caring for gerbils involves, of course, feeding and cleaning them which provide yet further opportunities for purposeful writing.

> The gerbils food smells like the gerbils cage and sawdust and I like the smell of the gerbils food. It feels soft but some bits were hard. It was rough. There's maize, nuts, cornflakes, oat pellets and sunflower seeds.

This closer examination of the food demonstrates simply the teacher's capacity to see learning potential in the straightforward everyday things. It is, though, precisely these straightforward everyday things that constitute the child's world. Slowing up the process sufficiently to take note of this and to respond to it is to heighten the significance of Zoe's own daily experience in her own eyes.

> *How to clean the gerbils out*
>
> First we get the bin and dust pan and brush then the clean sawdust. Then we took their toys out and we tipped the old sawdust in the bin. We put the clean sawdust in and their toys and then we put the gerbils in and their food and water. Then we put the dust pan away and sawdust away and the bin away.

The style and emphasis of the writing has changed to reflect a different purpose. Much of children's writing slips naturally from moments of personal observation to factual statement. In this case, however, there is no place for personal reflections. Instructions need to be sequential and economical. Zoe's appreciation of the purpose has provided the discipline for that change.

Incidental moments

The extension of the idea in children's, teachers' and parents' minds that learning, and writing as an element of learning, is not something confined within school walls is not achieved through public statement but in accepting the small, incidental opportunities that arise.

> When I took the gerbils home it was a struggle to get them in the car. Eventually we got them home. My sister was looking forward to the gerbils coming home, my mum was not looking forward nor was my dad . . . . The next day we had to take them back to school. I was sad.

There were several other short pieces in Zoe's completed topic along with drawings, paintings, prints and a clay model. The final piece was as follows:

> When Louise put her gerbil in he ran around and explored the cage. She named him Squeak. He is cuddly and soft and nice to hold. He has become used to his cage and he keeps running into his nest. A boy called Jason got some too. He called his Sweep and Sootey. They are nice too and they are cuddly and soft. When Miss Cook caught them she caught Jason's first then Louise's. Squeak was chewing up the bedding and Miss Cook said he is a fat one and Louise said yes and I agreed too but I did not say anything about it. Louise is going to take them home on Wednesday to stay and she said she was going to write home sweet home on the cage and on the outside of it she was going to write Squeak's home. When you shut the door it is all dark and dim.

This event, though far shorter in duration than the others she describes, produces her longest piece of written work. It is an incidental moment, but one that undoubtedly struck chords within Zoe, describing moments of intimacy and fun. It is so easy, while caught up with the pace of the day, for adults to take for granted the importance of such moments, the little things that do hold significance for the child and that in their recording are relived and perhaps explained to themselves.

The temptation is for the gerbils to take centre-stage. But it is what the gerbils have made possible that is of greater importance. All Zoe's written pieces stem from her activities, from her experience. The writing has provided the means for her to examine her experience. She has, at the same time, learnt about gerbils, about caring for them, their needs and characteristics.

The gerbils as experienced by upper junior children present yet more possibilities:

> We got a pair of scales, we put the male in the lefthand side and the female in the right side of the scale. The scales showed that the male weights 70 g. and the female weighs 50 g.

> *Which Food The Gerbils Like Best*
>
> I was trying to find out which food the gerbils liked best. I got an empty tray and five silver tops. I sorted some food out, I put eight nuts in one silver top. I put eight sunflowers in another, corn, cornflakes and food pellets. I put the silver tops in the tray but they just ignored the food, so I tipped the tops of feed into little piles on the floor, but they still kept ignoring the food and running away. So I got three pieces of card and glued them together. I put the piles of food on the floor and the card ring around but they kept getting out. So over-night I left the piles of food in the cage. I had a look in the morning and all the food had gone. I put some more food in the cage and left it for an hour. I found three nuts had gone out of the six I put in, no food pellets had gone, all the sunflowers had gone, five pieces of corn had gone. I did the experiment again to see if I got the same results. My graph shows the results.

Variety of purpose

> *My Graph*
>
> My graph shows the results of the food preference. I did the experiment twice to see if the results would be the same. The kind of graph I did was a non-rank order graph. When I coloured in the bars for my graph, for the first time I did the experiment I coloured the bars red. The second time I coloured the bars blue.

My Seeds

I put some sunflowers in a container and left them to soak over the weekend. There are fifty-five sunflowers in the container, they did not do anything except go soggy. I also put some pieces of corn in a container and left them to soak over the weekend. There are six pieces of corn which have started to get white roots. I left them for another two days, then I planted them. First I got two flower pots, and put some potting compost into the two pots, and put the seeds in the pots and covered them with the compost and watered them.

The Ill Gerbil

We found the male gerbil could not open his right eye, so we got some cotton wool and some warm water in a yogurt pot with a little drop of detol. We bathed it, dabbing it on with cotton wool. The next morning the gerbils cage was on the table, and Mr Mulligan told me he had found the gerbil dead and that he had disposed of it, I felt a bit shaky of the thought of the gerbil being dead. It did cheer me up a bit when Mr Mulligan said a boy was bringing another one in for us to have. We put the new gerbil in the cage with the female gerbil, they started to chase each other and fight. The female bit the new ones tail, and the little one bit the females head. The next day we got all the gerbils in the school together and kept swopping them around with our gerbils till we got a pair that did not fight.

The Gerbils Death

Our baby gerbils Captain, Tiger and Mischief died. First we found Captain had died we think of a broken back. So we decided to bury him. We took some sawdust, stones, a plaque of wood some trowels into the copse and we dug a hole near the fence for the grave. We filled in the hole and put sawdust on top and we lined it with stones and put moss around the edge. We wrote a name plaque for him it looked like this.

Captain a well known Friend
let him or her rest in Peace
Born 1982   Died 1982
RIP

The first time I spelt it all wrong and I had to rub it out. Soon after the other two gerbils died and we buried them one each side of Captain. Mark wrote one name plaque and John wrote the other. Their graves looked all the same and we felt very sad.

Our Maze

We made a maze to see which gerbil would take the shortest time to get out of the maze. First of all we got some long stripes of sugar paper. We made sure it was quite high. Then we folded the paper so it was Zig Zaggy when we opened it out. The first mistake we made was that the paper was not high enough. The other mistake was we didn't join the paper together with selloptape. When we had corrected them we put the Zig Zag stripes on the floor and we made a maze. Then we put the big gerbil in the maze and we timed how long it took him to find his way out it took him 55 seconds. Then we put the small gerbil in the maze and it took him 20 seconds. Then we did it again it took the big gerbil 60 seconds and the little gerbil took 30 seconds. I think the smallest gerbil was faster and cleverer and had a better sense of direction.

In these examples the children's writing has served a variety of purposes. The need to record the events over a period of time reinforced the importance of logical thought and disciplined notes and clarified for them what they had discovered. The use of the graph alongside the writing is incorporated as a further means of expression. The problem of the incompatible gerbils was not side-stepped. A real-life problem to be resolved. The written account was a summary of an experience that had taken quite some time and demanded considerable dialogue, organisation and co-operation. The reflective exercise of writing enabled the child to draw the main threads of the experience into a short coherent form, to provide, perhaps, a perspective of the experience.

There is no satisfactory substitute for being engaged in a 'genuine task'. The following two examples demonstrate precisely that.

There is no disguising the child's voice. In both examples the child is not describing the experience along with thirty-three other class mates, but is describing a personal experience, as it was for him. The attention to detail reflects the quality of children's observation. Such detail is only likely to be evident in the written report when the experience itself held significance for the child and when he believes, on the basis of previous experience, that what he has to say is valid and valued. Devising the maze has demanded of them vigorous thinking, sustained concentration and the resolution of difficulties. It was their complete involvement in a genuine task that led to the possibility of this articulate description.

These pieces of writing, like Zoe's, carry an authority that can only come as a consequence of personal experience. The authors of these pieces were, at that moment, 'the experts'. They had things to say that no one else was capable of saying. Whether engaged in a group or individual activity children should be using language for their own purpose and, in so doing, developing a confidence in their own voices. The teacher's task is to take these experiences and to co-opt the children's energy and enthusiasm in the service of their own needs. It is a mistake to believe that writing of quality will arise only from ambitious projects. The criterion is quite simply whether or not the task carries relevance and significance for the child.

Writing development

A continuous objective is for development; development in terms of the sophistication of the experiences and the way they are conducted, in the range and depth of skills brought to bear on them, of conclusions drawn and the learning attitudes and behaviours evident. Such development was evident in the increasing demands the children made of themselves in studying the gerbils. The skills allied to such growing demands can also arise within the activities of the children. It is in these moments that the best opportunities for teaching occur. The need, arising out of the task, creates the demand. The danger with the teaching of language rules and techniques is that they so easily become ends in themselves with excellence and control being sought for their own sakes. They are useful only in so far as they secure a product that is more faithful to the child's experience.

Joanna in year one (eight years) wrote:

> *Tortoisies*
>
> At school we have two tortoisies. The biggest one is called prince and the smallest one is called princess. Prince weighs 20 grams and 20 grams and another 20 grams and 200 grams and 1 kilogram and 50 grams and this is how they walk both of the tortoises walk in the same way first they put there front claws in front of them and push themselves along and this is how much princess weighs 500 grams and 50 grams and 200 grams 100 grams and 10 grams and 20 grams and another 20 grams and 1 kilogram what the tortoisies eat they eat lettces and tomotos and apples. Princesses shell is rough and princes shell is smooth when the cold winter days come the animals hibernate like dormouses and hegdogs and tortoisies and they wake up in spring and start collecting food for the long year ahead on Thursday we had a race with the tortoisies and prince won tortoisies have very hard shells to protect them from there enemy.

A year later (nine years) she wrote:

> *The tortoise*
>
> The tortoise has just woken up from hibernation. She is still a bit sleepy after her long sleep. She has a rough shell, it felt like a young trunk of a tree. She has thirteen sections of shell on ber back and 12 sections on her front. The tortoises scales are rough and are quite big on the head but as you go down the neck the scales become smaller. The tortoise uses the scales (like armour) for protection against its enemy. She has grown slightly bigger since I last saw her. When Miss Cook said Mr Barrett had a scheme for me I thought what scheme, then Miss Cook said go and get the tortoise from Mr Goldings area I thought it's going to be about my old topic, the one about tortoises. When I saw the tortoise it brought back some memories of when I was a first year when I was doing my topic. Last time I saw the tortoise it was last August which was a long time ago.

The development is evident in her vocabulary and in her sentence structure. It was also evident in her handwriting. It is not a development that has arisen from a slavish attention to 'English work' but rather a response to a growing need for articulacy and the constant use she makes of the written word to serve her own purposes.

The teacher's role in the writing task

Much of the children's writing which originates from first-hand experience is of a recording nature. The learning, by virtue of its doing, can be witnessed by the teacher. In this circumstance it is easier for the teacher to support the child in representing the experience faithfully. In the exploration of their experience, however, it is equally important that they should also engage in writing where the main effort is directed towards personal reflection. The teacher's role in this instance is infinitely more subtle. It is of paramount importance to understand the child's intentions. Indeed, as H. G. Wells commented, 'The forceps of our minds are clumsy things and crush the truth a little in the course of taking hold of it' (Koestler, 1984).

It is at this point that children's perception of their own viewpoint is critical. Unless children come to value their experience and to trust in their own voice what they produce is likely to be fake. Writing seriously and certainly in this context generally requires several drafts. To see this as a poor use of time is to diminish the role that writing has to play. Teachers must, as far as possible, help the child from within the experience. It is from this position that we are best able to judge the most appropriate moment for language development, for refining the form and extending the technical grasp. One approach is for the child, supported by the teacher, to identify the key elements of the experience. The key elements provide the points of reference in the succeeding drafts. The reverberation between those key elements and the written word help each effort move, stage by stage, from the gross to the refined, while at the same time remaining true to the original experience. In this context Kim (eleven years) wrote:

> **Guildford Cathedral**
>
> Quiet,
> Deadly,
> A threatening stillness,
> Row upon row of wooden chairs.
> Empty.
> Waiting for worshippers.
> Arches.
> Like rockets,
> Ready.
> On stand by for Heaven.
> A distant voice rebounding on the stone
> Staring walls.
> A Monster turned to stone by a wizard.
> A ghostly feeling comes over me.
> A lone person walks down the Aisle.
> Like a spirit fading away.
> The stone walls are like trees without branches.
> Deadly.
> Quiet.

Nevertheless, it is also true that the spontaneity, evident in some first drafts, is best left to carry its own conviction. Sunil's (ten years) response to a few moments sitting alone in the nave of Lincoln cathedral, while on a residential trip, falls into this category.

> Unexcited.
> No action.
> Everythings still.
> My heart beats slowly
> I am not used to big things.
> In my heart I feel strange.
> Small.
> Quiet.
> The Furniture Smooth and cold.
> Everything so still.
> Its so big
> it looks very empty.
> Everything is so big you cannot have enough time to
> look at the details.

There is also need to provide children with the opportunity of developing their inventive capabilities. This, too, springs from first-hand experience but that in which their imagination employs the known to create essentially new pictures or when they discard, for the duration of the task, given rules or assumptions and invent new ones. Kim's (eleven years) record of sitting alone in the Chapter House of Lincoln in part reflects this:

> **The Stone Weeping Willow**
>
> The Chapter House
> A stone weeping willow
> The trunk is huge
> The bark like thousands of snakes crawling
> up, forming branches that eventually fall
> to the ground
> On each side
> Between clusters of leaves
> Two great tears
> Roll to the ground
> Making a musty smell
> Like wet earth
> I want to find some-body
> To take me away from here
> I want to go home

Of all the other points that might be made the most pressing one would be that children should experience, in their activities and writing, a sense of fulfilment. Who could doubt that this was the case for Sarah (ten years) who concluded her topic by writing this:

> I am doing a project on our school wood and a little topic on the conservation area. I am doing a joint project between them. If you do not know much about these places I hope my book will help you to learn more about them. It was the best project I have ever done because it was fun and interesting. If you did this project I should think you will have as much fun and interest that I had.

Reference

Koestler, A., *Act of Creation*, Hutchinson, 1984, p. 383.

The dilemma of creative writing
Helen Arnold

The roots of children's will to write

Young children use spoken language quite adequately to fulfil their needs in the small community of home. At school they suddenly have to relate to many other people, to listen and respond in situations which are confusing and often frightening. They must find a language to accommodate these new contexts, a language which will refer mainly to real things and events around them – the requirements of the moment. Children quickly assume that the main purpose of 'school' language is to receive and transmit *facts* and *knowledge* – to be able to give *right* answers. Their first experience of 'proper' writing, occurring early in this new life, is the writing of their own names. Nothing, apparently, could be more factual than that. But even that act extends the experience of young children. To see their names on paper helps them to decentre, to stand outside themselves, thereby engendering a sense of pleasure and power. Gradually their expressive writing becomes a permanent record of experiences which were at first barely conscious. Through writing they begin to shape and control their outer world by relating it to their inner world. Personal writing for children, as for adults, is *partly intellectual and partly emotional*. Therein lies its importance, and the teacher, as reader, has to take both sources into account.

Paradoxically, just because they *are* young, children may be successful poets and story-tellers. Their response to sensory experience is more direct than that of most adults. They do not have to dredge through the accumulated silt of cognitive association and dead cliché. Spender (1955) said, 'The poet, above all else, never forgets sense impressions . . . particularly memories of early childhood.' Children's memories are being formed; far more of their experiences are new and exciting. They can bring them to the surface more easily, helped by the fact that the pattern of their thinking is more random, less bound by pre-existing conceptual frameworks. The teacher must value the loose and novel associations which children make, and help the writers to appreciate what they have done.

All children have curiosity – about themselves and others. Britton (1963) shows how very young children will listen to adults talking to each other, thereby taking a detached role, 'abstracted and ignored'. They are already taking on the *spectator* role, and can absorb not only the sequence of events which they are watching, but the moods and intonations that they hear. Untaught, they transform these into role-play for their peer-group audience. The cycle of listening and retelling is self-satisfying; there is no intention of impressing adults. Pleasure comes from the doing, for gossiping and storying about everyday happenings serve a universal human need. It is important that children should begin to write down these transformations of events, as well as talking about them, because in so doing they begin to shape experience. 'Literature is writing in the role of spectator – freed from the need of action or decision.'

When Elizabeth, at seven, wrote the following, she prefaced her work with the heading: 'This is not a story – this is the TRUTH'.

> When I was four then I had nearly dround myself and then my father came and said what is the matter and I said HELP! HELP! and he said I am comeing so he did and then I was saved and I learned to swim, and when I went home I had cakes and a drink and then I went to bed and then a few years later I was seven and I learned to swim. The end of my adventure'.

In spite of her insistence on the TRUTH of the episode, it seems clear that the recorded account is somewhat idealised, and that the whole event is seen as an 'adventure' worth recounting in a consciously created mode.

Marion, at the same age, feels free in her account to move backwards and forwards from the real to the unreal without explanation.

> Once I was walking along the road to church and I had my umbrella up because it was raining. It was very windy and suddenly the wind caught my umbrella and I floated right up in the air and sat on the wall. When its raining I like wearing my wellingtons because then I can go in puddles and my friend likes wearing his because he does not have to polish his shoes.

The first example shows also that the original events were unpleasant for Elizabeth, but in writing about them, making them into a story, she accommodated to the unpleasantness and actually enjoyed the telling. When she looks back on her experience it will have been contained and made less threatening because she wrote about it. Marion heightened the very ordinary wearing of wellingtons by juxtaposing them with a fantasy event. Young children, like all writers, not only select from experience in the retelling of events, but distort the facts to fit an artistic or a psychological purpose.

In responding to the writing, we must look at it *as a whole*, being particularly aware of the way in which the *selection* and *focusing* of events has, or has not conveyed an essence, a truth, which goes beyond the original experience – which manages it, in fact, through the medium of language. The initial selection of the events which are transformed in writing demonstrates a way of looking at the world, and may sometimes be a sad commentary. Andrew, at seven, wrote on one occasion:

> My daddy had pulled a head of a chicken

and this shortly afterwards:

> Last week I put my fist through the window on pupos.

David, at seven, wrote:

> I like the sun
> and the rain
> and the moon
> because the sun is yellow.

Whereas his classmate, an autistic child, wrote this:

> I like the moon
> I like the starrs
> because the sun is not out.

How shall we look at the writing?

It is when children in a class write on the same topic that the variety of treatment becomes striking, and we realise what remarkable powers of selection even young children have. Two children from a class of eight-year-olds who were asked to write about 'My house' demonstrate this.

Chris

> There are four people in my house. Helen, me, Mum and Dad. Helen is big for her age. She's tough and rough, and is scruffy. She hasn't much sense. I am tall, strong, a bit aggressive, quite intelligent. My mum is brainy, has curly hair, and is tall. My dad looks like Mick Mills and is tall strong and brainy.

Graham

> My house is semi-detached and it is red and it is next door to the Bull and so my Dad can go over for a drink. It has seven windows two toilets, and two bedrooms and five beds and two televisions, two lounges, one kitchen and four fireplaces.

The focus of these two writers is quite different; one thinks of his house as a collection of people and his impressions of those people, while the other makes an inventory of things. One is not more 'correct' than the other, but if one is considering which is a more total response, involving intellect and emotion, one might say that the first makes more impact. It becomes clear that some children will come much nearer than others to 'transforming' their experience in this way. The following three examples illustrate this further. They are all responses to the same topic 'Getting up in the morning'.

Clayton, aged ten

> In the morning my mum wakes me up then I go into the living room to eat my toast and drink my tea. When I get up I feel tired. I yawn then I go to the toilet. I clean my teeth with colgate tooth paste then I go to school.

John, aged nine

> I shoot out of bed like a bullet and all I hear is the bedclothes ruffle. I see my Lego car and start playing with it. I feel the rough edges with my fingers. I can smell very delicious bacon cooking. Then I come through to breakfast and eat it. I can feel the warm rough bacon on my tounge and then off in the cool air to school.

Helen, aged ten

> **Like a clockwork toy**
>
> As the sun appears through the curtains,
> It winds up my heavy key,
> Creak, creak, creak.
> I begin to stir.
> I twist and turn.
> Then I gradually
> Open my eyes,
> Lift my body,
> Then walk to the bathroom,
> Trot downstairs,
> Run to school.
> I'm at full speed now.

If we look carefully at these three pieces, we can make suggestions as to how the differences arise. Clayton's selection of events is inconsequential. Nothing really stands out as important or interesting to him. The 'thens' and 'ands' of the sentence construction reflect the loose, unconsidered associations, chosen mainly in temporal order. There is no clear beginning and ending, therefore little shaping or focusing on particular events and their relationship to each other. The experiences have not been reflected upon.

In discussion with the writer, it could be suggested that there are elements of interest which could be taken as a central focus – for instance, the statement 'When I get up I feel tired.'. Why? Boredom with the same repetitive tasks? Too many late nights? More generally, it seems that the writer does not really see much point, either for himself or an audience, in pursuing this subject. Another topic might interest him more. It could be that finding real purpose for his writing – publishing a class magazine, etc, would engage him more purposefully.

John's piece is 'well written', with an abundance of rather self-conscious imagery, perhaps reflecting his desire to please his teacher's instructions to use simile and – as Bullock put it – 'colourful or fanciful language, not "ordinary", using "vivid imagery"' (Bullock Report Chapter 11, Section 4). It does not seem, however, to show the engagement of true feeling. Here it will be more difficult to suggest gently that the writing might profit from more simplicity, from less conscious striving after effect. Again, the best practical way of helping might be to extract one sentence – perhaps the one which the writer himself chooses as being most real to him – and to start again from there.

Helen's poem must have involved reflection. Its extended metaphor is simply expressed, and genuine because of its simplicity and appropriateness. The length of lines, the short verbs, echo the awkwardness of initially 'getting going'. The loose associations have disappeared; experiences have been transformed into a unity. Did Helen realise what she had made? Her teacher must try to explain how the total poem has been successful, without making the writer too self-conscious about it. Perhaps this will be the most difficult task of all!

Form and content

We cannot look at even young children's writing in this way without becoming aware of how closely form and content are interlinked.

Rachel, aged nine

> I saw a man with his arms full of stars.
> He was puzzled about humans and their ways,
> He was in a hurry and was hot tempered.
> He didn't see me creeping through the darkness.
>
> The stars tickled his ears as he wandered.
> He gazed into space, still gripping tightly the stars;
> They were the crystals floating through his hands,
> And then gone for ever.
>
> If I had the chance to touch those crystals
> Which skim and slip and move,
> I definitely would touch them
> Before the shadows fall.

At this level of writing the content and form cannot really be dissociated, and we become aware of the interaction between sensory response, language and total experience. The poem would not mean the same in different language; the thought is special to that particular writer. We cannot even explain all of it to ourselves, but we feel it as a genuine experience of creation for the child. She must, even at nine, have considered the effect of the words, and the structure of the sentences.

Children include the visual pattern on the page in their awareness of form, which may be why they sometimes choose to write in poetry rather than prose. Kress (1982) shows how they have their own, predominantly visual, idea of a sentence, and equate lines on a page with units of meaning when they write. Certainly, Jacquetta, at six, seemed to be aware of the weightiness of managing content and form, when she wrote:

> I think I am going to make a sentence.

Even at an early age, children have a sense of form and rhythm, perhaps partly innate and partly developed from their early introduction to the highly patterned forms of nursery rhymes, playground chants and repetitive stories. They take pleasure in the distinctive features of words (rhyming, alliterating, etc), in puns and assonance and in the physical choice of where to put words on the page. They will experiment without direct instruction if they are encouraged to write short pieces or poems – a label they accept without suspicion. The sort of word-games which Brownjohn (1980) recommends are excellent ploys for reinforcing their natural love of playing with words. Here are three examples which show varied aspects of the effective use of word and form:

Jimmy, aged seven

> The cat's ears go down and when the ears go down . . . they cannot hear and they have got fear in their ears.

Patrick, aged seven

> I like the sea
> because it
> splashes
> walking
> in to
> the
> waves
> waves
> big.

Bryan, aged seven

> When I stroke my cat it feals as if I am pushing my hand along a brick wall.

These children are beginning to find their own voices in their writing. The words on the page echo their own physical voices, sounding in their heads as they write. The physical aspect of voice is important. Ted Hughes, speaking to an audience of Suffolk schoolchildren in 1982, said that poets begin to write with their own physical voice reverberating in their heads, and if later they depart from the reproduction of these natural rhythms, they are likely to become less good poets.

As children become more aware of other people's writing, they may struggle to use what they consider to be 'grown-up' language, and may lose, temporarily it is hoped, their own voices. We sense this in the following piece by an eleven-year-old boy, in which the effort for effect often over-rides the power of the natural voice.

> *Tadpoling*
>
> The tadpoles were out in their millions, masses of green slime, shoals of scum, with fragile rays of sunlight glittering through the clouds and illuminating the tadpoles, pond-skimmers restlessly gliding across the surface of the pond, the water mothering and housing all the creatures which rotated in its span. On the bank were frogs and toads, the frogs bounding about on polished emerald lilies and plunging through the surface mould into the dazzling underworld. Dragonfly darts jettisoned past, while I stood, my feet imbedded into the ground, my back arched over the water. Watching a shoal of tadpoles elegantly flitting along the water's base, unaware of there future fate. I cast the net down on them, punishing them for taking such pride in swimming under me. The ones which didn't swim away were put to shame in a bucket away from the delights of their own home.

This 'fine writing' would be very difficult to correct; it is accomplished – over-accomplished. It would probably be better for this writer to distance himself, for a time at least, from his own facility with words. He might try writing much more succinctly, in haiku form for instance, or to write for other than directly creative purposes. (Haiku is a form of poem originating in Japan, consisting of three lines; the first of five syllables, the second of seven and the third of five.) It might be possible for him to write some stories for younger children.

Sometimes children seem to pick up the idea that 'creative' writing must be esoteric and consciously 'poetic'. We must remember that it can be very down to earth and factual. The following extracts from Stephen's writing sum up more than any other examples, perhaps, what is valuable in children's personal writing. It is evident that the writing is not 'personal' or 'creative' in the accepted sense, nevertheless, it is full of associative linking which is unique to this child. The writing went on across a period of years, from age seven to about ten. There was no adult intervention, apart from interest. Stephen's uncle was a bus driver, and from that interest Stephen set up his own – imaginary – bus company, called Dunkurks. He concocted forms for the drivers to fill in, lapel badges, advertisements, letters and notices. He, as owner of the firm, began as S. Arthur Esq, later knighting himself (Sir Stephen Arthur) and finally achieving Lord Arthur. The poorly written and badly spelt early efforts became gradually more skilled, and typing took the place of writing. Above all, he transformed the ordinary happenings of his life to fit the project. A trip to Felixstowe docks led him to organise a time-table for his coaches to meet the ferries, a friend's cottage became a four-star hotel, with local walks and sights listed as its attractions. So a web of real associations became part of the self-perpetuating project.

Dunkurk's Coaches Ltd.
Date: 31 Oct 1980   Manager and Chairman   Sir Stephen Arthur

Dear Driver/Conducter,
              Hope you are well, and yore job will come in 1981 (summer
Yore driver/conducter Job No. and Licence No. will be
    196619   Yore licence runs out on the same date as you get it except
2 years later.

        please sign . . . .

            ricivd by

. . . .   to Sir Stephen Arthur

Dunkurks Travel Club

  If you would like to join the Dunkurks Travel Club all you have to do is to fill in the form below. A year's membership is £1.50. You will get a badge, a membership card & a letter 3 times a year called **THE TRAVELLER** with games, competitions & stories in it. You will also get 10 vouchers worth 50p each for traveling by Dunkurks (only 1 may be used at a time). You will also get a poster.

=====================   . . . .

MEMBERSHIP FORM

    Name/s . . . .

    Address . . . .

       age/s _____ number of people joining _____ £   p
                                               (money enclosed)

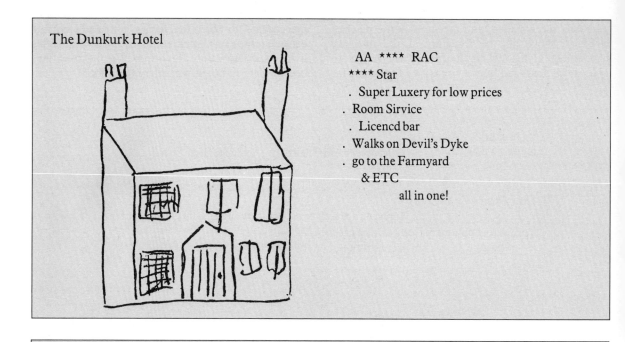

The teacher's part

One cannot, of course, teach creativity, in spite of the claims of the mind-flexing exercises which were popular in America in the 1960s. Nor is 'Use your imagination' a helpful suggestion. Creative outcomes arise from the myriad ways in which an individual collects and generates experiences. The task of expressing these associations in words is difficult, involves crafting, and may be helped by the teacher. We can begin by setting up an encouraging environment for self-expression. This hinges on two things – acknowledging that there are elements already present in children's minds which are worth drawing out, and building into the curriculum the opportunities for open-endedness.

More specifically, there are ways to help children to find their own voices.

- Talk with them. Resist the temptation of feeding in too many ideas, and lists of colourful vocabulary. Perhaps continue for longer than usual the infant teacher's method of writing down conversation and 'what they want to say'. Ideally this would be on an individual basis, but group and class discussion on the same lines has the advantage of spawning ideas from shared experience. The aim is to tap their own interests, rather than to provide stimuli which we as adults think 'poetic'.

- A seemingly contradictory approach, which will nevertheless complement what for some children is too great a freedom, is to provide fairly tight constraints on the form of writing. Haiku and similar compact, carefully limited structural forms encourage careful thought about every word – since there are not many of them! Shape and concrete poetry allow for conscious visual patterning. A seemingly limited topic like 'Boxes' can, surprisingly, provoke a witty response.

A girl aged eleven

> **Boxes**
>
> You put me in a box
> Marked horrid
> Because I say things I shouldn't,
> But I cannot help it.
> They come out like a gust of wind.
> You put me in a box called clever.
> I have my problems the same as you do.
> You only do that because I put my hand up
> And answer questions.
> You think I am a face that you see every day
> And that is all, just a face.
> You put me in a box named little bookworm
> Because I read a lot.
> I only read because I like reading.
> Some people put me in the kind box
> But I do not think I am kind, because I get angry.
> I put you in a box named silly.

So the first suggestion calls for free-flowing association; the second focuses attention on the surface features of the language, and shows how the struggle to find the right words and structures need not be limiting.

- From the earliest stages build in the belief that the *re-working* of ideas is worthwhile, that the first rough jottings are entirely free, but that the finished product is worth a great deal of re-drafting. Children should keep a small notebook for jottings and sketches where anything that interests them can be collected as raw material for future writing. They will begin to see the value of giving time for the unconscious to work – the artist's 'incubation period'. 'Real' authors' notebooks and drafts could form interesting models.

- Share written work. Encourage children to read their work aloud to each other. Publish it in class magazines, wall newspapers, taped presentations. The concept of writing for a known audience is important.

Not every piece of writing will be, or should be, creative. When it does occur, however, it must be appreciated, and the children must know that their work has been read with pleasure – for the reader's appreciation is partly intellectual, partly emotional, just as the writing was. Techniques of writing are important, but will develop only if children *need* to say something. Evaluation should be a shared enterprise, with the children gradually contributing equally to the discussion of why something in their writing did or didn't work for the reader.

In order to elicit an aesthetic experience it seems that there must be an engagement of feeling, with a heightened awareness of that feeling, for which the most apt verbal expression has to be found. The feeling will rarely be expressed by direct definition, but by bringing subconscious associations to the level at which they can be consciously linked to events. As we have tried to demonstrate in the examples, this will be evinced partly in the choice of words, and partly by an underlying unity of attitude which will encapsulate the total experience. The fact that children naturally respond *affectively* as well as *cognitively* is therefore to be valued.

Examples have been given of writing which can be read aesthetically, but in practice few teachers evaluate even personal writing in this way. They are not often genuinely interested in the quality of the writing in relation to the content, but concentrate more on the mechanical skills; they hesitate to criticise on 'literary grounds', tending to evaluate according to what to expect from a particular child at a particular time.

Concerning this dilemma, Britton (1963) wrote as follows.

> Teachers are coming to realise that imaginative writing and creative responses are essentially part of one process: that the more fully you understand the nature of each, the more they come to resemble one another at heart: and that in practice, to see them as distinct or separate activities is damaging to both.

One of the main aims of asking children to write should be that in analysing their own processes and products they will be more able to appreciate the writing of others. One of the main aims of reading to them and encouraging them to read good writing for themselves is to help them with the development of their own writing. Often little connection is made between the 'creative writing' session and what is read and painstakingly 'comprehended' in pages of exercises. Children do not know how to evaluate their own work, or indeed, how the teacher evaluates it. More important, they do not know how to *feel* about it. 'Creative' writing is not just a conditioned response to stimuli; it is a complicated act which must be discussed, as far as possible, with children from the earliest stages. If it is worth doing, it is worth talking about.

Gombrich (1960) says, 'Whereas dreams and images are solitary activities, Art is essentially social. It has, moreover, a history, a style, in contrast to perception and dreaming.' Children would be capable of learning this appreciation if it were developed from an early stage with reference to their own work.

The value of 'instant response' is firmly entrenched in school life. The child who puts up his hand first is the one who is chosen to answer. There is little opportunity to work through the natural, slow processes of creation – the collecting of experiences, the period of incubation, the reflection. Children might well discuss together how they actually set about getting ideas, drafting and redrafting. Writing, however, tends in practice to be carried out to order, and to be accepted or rejected with scant comment. That it can be otherwise is seen when visiting authors help children to develop a readiness to become craftsmen, to reword and rethink – and it can be seen happening then with children of all levels of ability.

It may be difficult to think of children's writing as an aesthetic product, but it has been shown that it often warrants such serious reception. Children should perhaps be asked to write *less*, but more *importantly*.

All examples of children's writing are unpublished work, collected by the author from schools in Cambridgeshire and Suffolk between 1963 and 1982.

References and recommended reading

Britton, James, *Studies in Education: the arts and current tendencies in education*, published for the University of London Institute of Education by Evans Bros Ltd, London, 1963.

Britton, J., *et al*, *The Development of Writing Abilities*, Macmillan, London, 1975.

Brownjohn, S., *Does It Have to Rhyme?*, Hodder & Stoughton, London, 1980.

DES, *Children and Their Primary Schools*, HMSO, 1957.

DES, *A Language for Life*, HMSO, 1975.

Gombrich, E., *Art and Illusion*, Phaidon, London, 1960.

Kress, G., *Learning to Write*, Routledge & Kegan Paul, London, 1982.

Langdon, M., *Let the Children Write*, Longmans, London, 1961.

Marcuse, H., *The Aesthetic Dimension*, Macmillan, London, 1977.

Spender, S., *The Making of a Poem*, Hamish Hamilton, London, 1955.

5

Organising writing together
Irene Farmer

Several aspects of organisation need to be kept in mind as we try to promote children's writing development, that is, to encourage the gradual move towards greater fluency, greater differentiation and the choice of greater complexity.

The first two organisational aspects are outside the writing. They provide the environment in which the writing takes place and will be touched on briefly in relation to particular scripts. They are the creation of an enabling climate and the physical organisation of space and time. Examples of the sorts of factors that teachers may wish to use to create a positive environment for writing may be seen in the boxes opposite. While the majority of classes operate within constraints of timetabling and resources, most teachers will be able to provide some of the factors that can help to create a positive environment for writing, some of the time.

The third aspect of organisation we need to be aware of is inside the writing itself and is the main focus of this chapter. Why do teachers need to be aware of the underlying structures in children's writing? There are several good reasons.

Structures vary both in type and in levels of complexity, and will differ for different kinds of writing. Awareness of structures will help us to be *alert to the demands* that different types of writing are likely to make on younger or less able writers and to plan our programmes of work accordingly.

At the same time, ability to analyse underlying structures will help us to *recognise the achievements in thinking* in even comparatively humble pieces of writing, where meaning may be masked by lack of skill in the surface features such as poor handwriting or spelling.

In addition, knowledge of structures should enable us to *intervene helpfully* where syntax falls down and meaning becomes unclear, by revealing to children the underlying structure of the material they are working with, and thus helping them with the thinking, rather than simply correcting the superficial errors.

Finally, we can sometimes help children to build the structure in *advance* of the writing, helping them to *shape their own thinking* as they impose order on material, and then use this ordering as a plan for their writing.

Examples of factors which help to create an enabling climate

Giving children the chance to –

- choose what they want to write about;
- work with an idea or theme over time;
- work in different media in addition to words;
- consult each other and a teacher;
- return to earlier drafts and reshape them;
- present their work to an interested audience.

Examples of organisation of space and time

Grouping furniture and resources in a variety of ways to permit a variety of ways of working such as –

- individual and small group research and reading;
- teacher reading to class;
- painting and modelling;
- role play with teacher in role;
- tape recorders available for recording and listening;
- individual and small group writing;
- stationery for drafting and final drafts;
- individual and small group conferences with teachers;
- individual and small group presentations.

Although the ideas presented in this chapter are appropriate to the consideration of writing from people of all ages, the examples will be drawn from writers in the junior years, of ages nine to eleven.

Where to start?

A strong starting point for children's writing is stories based on their own experience. All of us have a fund of anecdotes which we enjoy retelling, sharing the fun or the sorrow, the delight or remorse. Even at its simplest, this retelling requires a careful selection of appropriate detail and information in the light of our perceptions of needs of audience and situation. Nevertheless, often the story can be retold more or less as it happened. The incident itself provides a chronological order to be interwoven with known settings and characters. More mature writers can create variations of the chronological order, such as branches in the plot (for example, 'Meanwhile, down in the woods . . .'), or flashbacks (for example, by starting in the hospital bed and returning to the scene of the accident). They might also incorporate a running commentary comparing and contrasting their thoughts and feelings at the time of the event, with those of now, in retrospect. So, even within personal narrative, varying degrees of complexity are possible.

However, what happens when children are required to leave the known, the story based on their own first-hand experience, and venture into the unknown, stories based on imagined people, events and places? What resources are available to children when they have to create, rather than recall, the characters and what happens to them?

Not unnaturally, young writers will have to rely on ideas from television, their reading, and stories they have heard, and may produce imaginary stories based on stereotypes to simplify planning. Many teachers will also be familiar with the imperfect selection of what to put in – endless descriptions of getting dressed and having breakfast, or long-winded dialogue about inviting friends out to play, or endings such as 'and I woke up and told my mum all about my dream', safe but highly predictable.

A crucial form of support therefore is for children to hear, read aloud, a wide variety of short or long stories and poems, and articles from reference books, magazines and newspapers. As well as enjoying the communication in its own right, this will provide the major means by which young or less fluent readers may gradually absorb a variety of written styles and structures. Apart from this long-term incidental learning we can also deliberately feed in models for particular pieces of writing, though this pre-planning need not always be made obvious to the children. In the example that follows, two children of very different levels of writing ability are able to draw on resources offered by the same model to produce their own imaginary stories.

Boffy stories

The class teacher had been reading the *Boffy* stories (Barry 1971), usually one each day. The children

Mark, aged nine

November 23rd BOFFY and the magic ring

One day BOFFy was in the garden with Jeny Jeny and BOFFy was diging he hit Something with his Spade it was a bottle with a ring in it he got the ring out. it was very Small he put it in is pocket he told Jeny Jeny She Said it was a ear-ring but it as not got a Fastner he carid on diging he hit something another bottle a fairy was in the bottle boffy said Jeny Jeny I have Found Anther bottle She came over to him She saw the little Fairy She said "the ring must belong to the Fairy She is still alive" The Fairy said "have you got a ring?" "Yes" said Jeny Jenny and the Fairy said "iF you Give you Five wishes each ooh" "Yes" said BOFFy and Jenny They Gave the ring back to the Fairy She said "Give these people Five Wishes each and She Flated away in the sky like a bee or a wasp They thought what to do with the Five wishes Boffy wished For a Microscope Jenny wished for a bike BOFFy Said I will wish for a bike too but it will be a BMX Bike and Jenny Jenny said "I will have a Pram BOFFy said I will Give a wish For my dad he would like a car Jenny Jenny said my dad would like a car too BOFFy said my mum would like a video Jenny Jenny said my mum would wish for a video" So She wished for a video For her mum They had one more wish left BOFFy wished for ten hundred pounds Jenny Jenny wished For ten hundred pounds too They got their wish BOFFy got a microscope Jenny Jenny got her Bike BOFFy got is BMX Bike Jenny Jenny got her Pram Boffys dad got his car Jenny Jennys dad got his car too and boFFys mum got her caravan Jenny Jennys mum got a video and boFFy ten hundred prunds Jenny Jenny got her ten hundred prounds they kept on diging but they did not Find a bottle agan Their mum and dad was pleased about a car a caraven and Jenny Jennys mum and dad was pleased too they played on their Bikes and BOFFy made a good use of is microscope and Jenny Jennys pram she always plays with her pram went she goes out.

enjoyed the stories, because of the outlandish situations, the obvious humour and because, at nine, they were old enough both to identify with Boffy, and to feel slightly superior to him.

The central idea of the stories is that Boffy is only a little boy, about six years old, small and physically weak, who does not understand sarcasm, but who is a 'self-confessed genius'. He is an inventor extraordinaire whose efforts to help people invariably go wrong, usually ending with an irate father and a sore behind!

When the last *Boffy* story had been read aloud, the children were disappointed until they realised that they could write their own. Thus there was the combination of an appreciative audience, a ready-built character and setting (which the children knew quite well by then) and a well rehearsed format, that is, a beginning, in which there is an attempt to help in some way, a middle, in which things go wrong, and the inevitable conclusion. Within the class, children used their options in various ways. Some stayed very close to the setting and characters of the model. Others chose to retain the sequence of the plot, while others, like Mark, for instance, decided to keep the characters but to place them in a new situation (see page 34).

As the children's 'Boffy' stories were read out (a few each day) the class reacted with satisfaction and pleasure, and Mark took his well deserved credit along with the others. From hearing Mark's story read aloud, one would hardly suppose that a few months earlier he had had a 'Reading Experience Age' of only 6.9 years and his writing had been like that of average seven-year-olds!

How has Mark used his opportunity? Superficially, this is by far the longest piece he had managed to write up to this time, the third month of the Autumn term. What has he managed to do in this increased length? We notice his beginning and ending, 'One day Boffy was in the garden with Jenny Jenny . . . She always plays with her pram when she goes out.' and acknowledge that Mark has so far assimilated the linguistic conventions of stories as to be able to use them appropriately and with fluency. He uses speech for the first time in his writing so far to indicate the characters other than Boffy. In several places he presents logical reasoning within the tale, sometimes implicitly, sometimes explicitly. For example, 'She said it was an ear-ring, but it has not got a fastener' draws on the direct personal knowledge Mark has of ear-rings, wearing one himself when not at school. The implicit reasoning here is that the found ring cannot be an ear-ring *because* it has not got a fastener.

Secondly, Mark writes, 'She said, "The ring must belong to the fairy she is still alive." The fairy said, "Have you got a ring?"'. Again, the connection is implied. Next, we see Mark in disguise, using the hypothetical, although the syntax falls down a bit – 'the fairy said, "If you give (me the ring then I will give) you five wishes each."'. Here we notice the conventional literary associations discussed by Applebee (1978), as Mark exploits shared expectations about fairies, their size, their 'goodness', their ability to survive in unlikely places and their ability to grant wishes.

For the five wishes themselves, Mark seems to rely on structures absorbed from his early reading books, his most frequent reading material. He manages to keep them in sequence, and to repeat them in sequence, which simplifies the necessary planning while extending his story. He is probably drawing on sources such as *Goldilocks and the Three Bears*, *The Three Billy Goats Gruff* and folk tales such as *Tom Thumb*, where three wishes are involved. He might also have drawn his idea of the fairy in the bottle from the Arabian Nights' story of the genie imprisoned in a bottle. As for the choice in the wishes, we recognise that what he wished for was not typical of Boffy, apart from the microscope, but typical of Mark himself!

Another convention that Mark usefully exploits in his ending is the repetition of an earlier phase of the story, 'they kept on digging but they did not find a bottle again.'. The additional repetition of each person and each family being pleased with the presents Boffy and Jenny Jenny had wished for them, and Boffy's 'good use of his microscope' leads to a satisfying and familiar conclusion. This repetition is frequently used in the model, as in many stories for younger children. For Mark it has the advantage of adding appropriate length without putting additional burdens on his planning capacity.

Throughout, Mark has managed to maintain a persistent stance as narrator, creating the 'spectator' role for himself and his reader. It is, perhaps, just the beginning of a move towards Britton's 'poetic' category, in the sense of being a shaped and complete story, (Pradl, 1982).

Joe, a much more able reader and writer than Mark, has also gained from absorbing features from the model over time. We find new developments for Joe as a writer, as he successfully combines and interweaves five separate structural elements (see page 36).

Like the other children, Joe takes on the role of narrator, writing in the third person and in the past tense. From this position he is able to tell his readers of both external and inner events. He bases his structure on several elements:

1 *The passage of time*

'One day . . . after a while . . . when he got home . . . he was just about . . . had to got to bed . . . in the morning . . . then went to school . . . at the end of school . . . in about half an hour . . . just about to test . . . when Mrs Smith . . . just then.'

Joe, aged nine

November 23rd Boffy and the electric dog

One day Boffy was walking home from school and began to think and after a while he noticed he was quite lonely. When he got home he thought he would invent a pet for himself so he thought which pet he would like a cat, a hamster, a rabbit, a budgie, or a dog. Well, a cat has funny eyes so I wont have that and a hamster is too little and has very sharp teeth and a rabbit just sits there and eats. A budgie just sits on a perch and sings and Boffy hates singing! Now a dog you can train because it walks and can do alsorts of good things like tricks and climbing so Boffy decided to invent a dog. So he was just about to go into his shed when there was a shout: "BOFFY COME HERE!" It was Mr. Smith. "What's the idea of trying to sneak out its hours after your bedtime" "sorry dad" replyed Boffy just then Mrs. Smith came downstairs and helled at Boffy "whats all the shouting about" "nothing mum" moaned Boffy and had to go to bed without any supper. In the morning it was Monday and so he got dressed had a wash and went to clean his teeth and went to have a piece of toast and a glass of milk and then went to school. At the end of school he rushed home dropped his bag in the kitchen and rushed to the shed he got tin, nails, tubes, string, wires, rope, and started to work. In about half an hour he he came out with his tin dog on rope. Boffy looked very pleased with himself there were 10 buttuns fast, slow, start, stop, forwards, backwards, left, right and on, and off, Boffy was just about to test it when "yoo hoo" it was jenny jenny what are you doing? she said "I'm testing my pet want to help?" said Boffy "OK" she said so Boffy switched it on and it moved perfectly "Yahoo" yelled Boffy "isn't it great?" "yes very" squealed Jenny Jenny with excitement just then Jenny Jennys mum shouted "Jenny Jenny bedtime", "alright mum" Jenny Jenny replyed. Now Boffy can be very forgetful and he forgot to switch the dog off and this dog liked to eat wood and it ate right through the wood of the shed. Mr. Smith heard the noise and picked up a piece of wood to clobber the thing with, the dog smelt rotten wood on the compost heap so he neared it and Mr. Smith tripped over the dog and went head first into the compost heap. When Mrs. Smith heard the fuss she went downstairs soon followed by Boffy. Only Boffy knew how to control the dog so he ran up to the dog and switched it off. Just then his dad grabbed him by the arm and smacked him and he got sent to bed with no supper and no pocket money for the next six months because of the shed.

2 *The external events*

'was walking home . . . go into his shed . . . had to go to bed . . . got dressed . . . milk . . . went to school . . . rushed . . . dropped . . . rushed . . . started to work . . . came out . . . test . . . moved perfectly . . . forgot to switch the dog off . . . ate right through . . . Mr Smith heard the noise . . . to clobber the thing with . . . dog smelt . . . neared it . . . Mr Smith tripped . . . went downstairs . . . followed by . . . knew . . . ran up to . . . switched . . . grabbed . . . smacked . . . sent to bed.'

3 *The inner events*

'Began to think . . . noticed . . . thought he would invent . . . so he thought . . . just sits on a perch and sings . . . decided . . . only Boffy knew.'

4 *The speech of Boffy, his parents and Jenny Jenny*

'BOFFY, COME HERE! . . . what's the idea . . . hours after your bedtime . . . Sorry dad . . . what's all the shouting . . . ', etc. (A much wider vocabulary than previously is used to indicate speech: 'shout . . . it was Mr Smith . . . replied . . . yelled . . . moaned . . . it was Jenny Jenny . . . said . . . yelled . . . squealed . . . shouted . . . replied' which suggests progress in itself.)

5 *Authorial comment*

'Boffy hates singing . . . Now a dog you can train because it walks and can do all sorts of good things like tricks and climbing . . . Now Boffy can be very forgetful . . . this dog liked to eat wood.' Joe's authorial comment is a very sophisticated technique. It allows the writer three positions in relation to the reader and the characters.

i. As a narrator of events.
ii. As one seeing inside Boffy's mind and reporting his inner speech.
iii. As one cueing the reader to things about Boffy and the situation that the reader would not otherwise know.

These three modes permit the writer to keep a safe distance from the events and release him from any responsibility for them. If anything goes wrong, after all, it's Boffy's fault!

Within these five structural elements are various sub-structures and new writerly devices which you might like to explore for yourself. However, even without further acknowledgement, it is clear that having a well-rehearsed model and a ready-made, enthusiastic audience helped both children to attempt things in their imaginative stores that had been outside their previous written range.

Towards extending their range

While it is hard for young or less able writers to maintain consistently four or more strands through the length of a fictional story, most transactional writing is even more difficult for them. Here, they are likely to be dealing with times, places, events or processes remote from their daily experience. This in itself may involve a great deal of imaginative effort. In addition, often the new information will not have an inbuilt chronological order, so other ways of organising it will have to be created. At the same time, pupils will be having to put themselves into a new role in relation to their readers, formal, impersonal and objective, with the aim of informing or persuading rather than of sharing. Britton *et al* (1975) have discussed the ambiguities inherent in this role, where the reader is not likely to be someone interested in the new information (as a group of peers could be) but a 'teacher-as-examiner' whose main concern is to check the correctness of already known facts.

To illustrate the effect of these demands on the young writer, let us look at three pieces of writing by eleven-year-old Julie. Her teachers had provided the tremendous support of an ongoing project in the humanities, with the whole year group participating. Picture to yourself a wing of a purpose-built middle school, with fairly open classrooms surrounding a shared carpeted area, a utility area with water and work benches, and corridors lined with display boards. Everywhere you look are scenes of Red Indian life, books with pictures, poems and stories; models, paintings and writing produced by the children; a wigwam two metres high, patterned with authentic designs; and many informative displays supporting the projects of individuals or small groups.

Some children are working together, scanning reference books for information related to their chosen topic, noting down key words and then attempting to summarise in their own words the material gleaned from several sources. Others are listening to a small group presentation on a particular aspect, while other individuals are reading, writing or drawing. Yet, even with this wealth of available information, accessible through a variety of media, and with an enthusiastic audience ready to respond to her findings, Julie has difficulty in moving from the stance of narrator to that of informer. Here, first, is her story:

Julie, aged eleven *First draft*

> *Buffalo Hunt*
>
> When I was very young I got taken from my parents by Comanches. There was nothing I could do. When I got older I begun to like them. But it seemed hard work.
>
> I saw men hunting. They ~~was~~ were very brave. Then my chance came to hunt my first time ever. I got a pure white horse to ride. I called him Thunder. He galloped like the swift or wind.
>
> ~~My arrows~~ Then I got all my arrows. As the men made them we had to go and get them. Then we we rode of for the Buffalo.
>
> (Then) When we saw them together, We galloped in to a semi cicle. Then the buffaloes started to ~~rage~~ rage then they started running. Then we galloped. We were very excited. But we had to catch a buffalo. Then I hit a buffalo. He reared with rage but then fell to the ground dead. We had been on horse back all day. We ~~caughted~~ counted up how many buffaloes we had caught. I caught three buffaloes. I was very proud of myself. ~~Th~~ But big chief wise Owl said, "Never be proud till you have caught 6 ~~buffa~~ buffaloes single handed." We had a great big feast round a blazing fire. I thought about what ~~cheif chief wise~~ wise had Owl said. (But) I thought he would ~~of~~ have been proud of me. (But) I forgot about it and watched the feast.

Imaginative narrative includes many features that nine-year-olds (and some thirteen-year-olds) find difficult. Julie copes with a long time span, effectively centring on the hunt itself and the feast afterwards. She takes on the narrator role from the point of view of a captured boy and maintains this stance quite convincingly, especially as she incorporates in the role both commentary ('There was nothing I could do... But it seemed hard work.') and reflection ('I was very proud of myself. But big chief wise Owl said, "Never be proud..." ... I thought about... I thought he would have been proud of me.').

In passing, we observe that within imaginative narrative Julie is beginning to monitor her writing while she writes, correcting the grammar ('was' changed to 'were', 'of' to 'have'), deciding how to explain about the arrows being made and then collected, changing 'Th' to 'But' to emphasise the contrast between her own pride and Chief Wise Owl's view of it, instead of simply continuing the story chronologically with 'Then', and correcting her own spelling, changing 'pround' to 'proud' and 'cheif' to 'chief'. There may be an indication of the planning needed for even a comparatively simple story like this one, as we see 'caughted' corrected to 'counted', followed by 'caught' later in the sentence. The story also relies on a considerable amount of information about Red Indians and their customs.

What happens when Julie is asked to convey information separately from its context of character and events?

Julie, aged eleven *First draft*

> *Why I think buffalo was so important to the Indian?*
>
> The tail of the buffalo was used for rope.
>
> The skin of the buffalo was used for skin mocasins and all so shields.
>
> The hooves of a buffalo was made for glue.
>
> The big horns of a buffalo could be made for spoons and gunpowder pouches.
>
> The buffalo bones were made move muscil intrumens.

We see that Julie sensibly selects the most basic of all forms of conveying information, the list. But while this reduces the burden of planning a reasoned response to the question 'Why?', it leaves her without an obvious structure. The ordering in the list may be quite arbitrary. Should she start with the tail and move along the buffalo to its head? Or should she try to group the artefacts under headings such as clothes, utensils, etc, and then try to arrange these in a logical order, governed by an over-riding principle such as necessity for life? She decides to say what each part of the buffalo is used for, leaving the importance implicit, and starts off confidently enough. However, by the third line, the sub-structure she has created for herself

'The *x* of the buffalo *was used for*....'

breaks down. You don't *use* hooves for glue. You *make them into* glue. But only part of this new construction appears on the paper, while 'made for' becomes the revised template. The struggle is particularly apparent in the last line where she loses her safe beginning, transforming it into 'The buffalo bones were made...' and nearly losing the sense of '... into musical instruments.'

We can see from the context of the story and the list that in this case it is not the information that is giving Julie problems, though much of the material in subjects such as environmental studies or science may be conceptually difficult. Her difficulties are caused by the demands of the task – creating an order, taking on the role of instructor, writing in a formal style and, ideally, arguing an explicit case by showing a need that could not be met in any other way, while at the same time keeping out any subjective ideas or feelings of her own. That she has such feelings is clear from her poem, where the freedom from an imposed form has given Julie the chance to express a mood and a viewpoint, in a kind of chant or lament for the passing of the Indians and the buffalo:

Julie *Final draft*

> *Dusk cleared tribe with buffalo*
>
> Feathers flew
> Bones rot.
> Under the hilltop where sunrise comes
> Tribes and warriors lay in peace.
> Down near the riverside the buffalo lay
> Cannot be used for anything more.
> So let them lay in peace.
> Let feathers go
> Let bones rot
> Let them live in peace.
> The dusk passed
> The sunshine passed
> So has rain
> So they haunt
> Don't worry
> They will not hurt anymore.
> They live in peace
> With animal
> With person.
> They live in peace.

It is the opportunity to write in a variety of styles, with differing underlying structures, that has allowed Julie to share with her peers and teachers some of what she knows and feels about the Red Indian.

Supporting gradual differentiation in children's writing

One way of helping young writers to move towards a more transactional style is to work out, with the class or small group, a series of questions, the answers to which will form the basis of the writing. The group of nine-year-olds who wrote the 'Boffy' stories had been working on a major project 'All about me', based on the Schools Council's Health Education Project called 'Think well'. The children had brought photographs of themselves as babies, run identification competitions and were engaged in a variety of activities such as measuring each other, painting, drawing and modelling, observing a mother wash her baby's hair and change its nappy, reading, and watching related television programmes. Recognising the increased demands, one class teacher tried also to give her children a strong base in personal knowledge, as they attempted a more informative written style. The questions the children worked out together will seem obvious to most adults, but it was the children who thought of them, arranged them in a logical order (still partly based on time) and who had to ask at home to find out the answers.

Me as a Baby
When were you born?
Where were you born?
What did you weigh when you were born?
Did you have hair and teeth when you were born?
What were your first words?
How old were you when you started to walk?

Here we see Mark, whom we have met before, relying extensively on both the questions and their form. He chooses to start his answer to almost every question on a separate line. Eventually, this idea of starting a new line for a new topic is likely to help him with paragraphing as he becomes able to elaborate sufficiently to make paragraphing necessary.

Mark, aged nine

> *September 16th Me As A Baby*
> I was born on a Monday Morning at 7.55 On the Seventh of May 1973.
> I was born at Poplar dive Crigglestone. I wayhed eight pounds when I was born.
> I had plenty of hiar but no teeth When I was born.
> My frist word was mum and dad.
> I Started to walk when I was elevn months old.
> My mum says I was a good baby some times.

That he succeeds at all is due to his ability to simplify the planning involved. He does this by using the 'I was born' motif for four out of seven sentences, instead of verbs like 'got' and 'went' which had been prevalent in his earlier (story) writing. In the remaining three sentences, he uses 'when I was', 'I was' and 'was', keeping his selection of verbs to a minimum, while he struggles with the following problems.

Letter forms.
Lack of fluency in handwriting.
Spelling systems.
The inability to scan back to keep track of
– what's been said
– the tenses
– the stance to reader.
The inability to read with expression, thus lacking the intonation to help with
– recognition of sentence endings,
– punctuation.

However, he extends his informative stance in the last line by using reported speech to add relevant information: 'My mum says I was a good baby some times.', which also stands as a summary. We might take this up with Mark orally – 'What did you do when you were a good/bad baby, Mark?' We need to be alert to any changes in structure, selection of verbs, or new ways of linking that a child may use in order to extend or elaborate new meanings.

Yvonne, coming between Mark and Joe in her ability as a writer, reduces the demands of the new form by using 'and' and dwelling on the temporary disability she was born with. Thus her report becomes more of a narrative towards the end.

Yvonne, aged nine

> *September 16th Me As A Baby*
> I was bron at 8 Hilltop Diver on the 31st of Jaunary 1973. I was bron on a Wednesday morning at four o'clock and I weigh eight pounds twelve ounces. I had a little bit of black hair and no teeth. I Started to walk when I was ten months old. My mum was cald when I started to walk because I had to where a splint on my hips since I was bron and my legs used to sik out at the sides I had to go to the hosbatal for a long time.

Like Mark, Yvonne relies on the questions for her order, though she extends their basic form by incorporating a variety of connectives.

I was born at ... on ...
I was born on ... at ... and I (weighed) ...
I had a ... and (no teeth).
I started to (walk) when ...
... was (glad) when

I started to (walk) because
I had to (wear) . . .
I was born and (my legs)
used to . . .
I had to go to . . . for . . .

Again we see repetition of the sentence structures helping Yvonne to keep control over her information. She enables us to share in her mum's gladness when Yvonne started to walk, through involving us in her mum's reasoning, 'My mum was glad when I started to walk because I had to wear a splint on my hips since I was born and . . .'.

Joe also makes use of the informative structure suggested by the questions, using 'was' and 'had' and 'when' predominantly.

Joe, aged nine

> *September 16th Me as a baby*
>
> I was born on Thursday May 24th at a quarter to ten in the morning at Ellison Memorial hospital in Oakley it was a very hot day. I was the biggest baby in the hospital. I weighed nine pounds. I had lots of hair it was cut 3 hours after I was born to stop it getting in my eyes. I was a good and quiet baby. I was awake a lot. Julie made me do hand stands when I was ten days old. I started saying yaya, (my grandmother). I started to walk when I was 1 year old. I took my first steps in the bedroom floor. I was very greedy and ate until I had tummyache.

He also incorporates much extra information. For example, as well as telling us his weight, he includes a comparison, 'I was the biggest baby in the hospital.'. We are intrigued by the information that his sister Julie made him do hand stands when he was ten days old, and would like to know more about the incident – especially mum's reaction! The incorporation of the bracketed aside 'yaya (my grandmother)' suggests a strong sense of audience and understanding of audience needs, especially as he did not feel it necessary to explain who Julie was. It also demonstrates Joe's command of a useful, and fairly advanced, writer's technique.

A series of questions then, preferably arising from the children's own curiosity and interests, can provide a skeleton which the children can use to a greater or lesser extent, as they attempt to write in a less familiar mode.

Questions as keys to reference work

One of the most difficult things for children (and older students) to do is learn how to extract information from books. All too often they end up copying material that, at worst they don't understand, and at best they have had little active involvement with. There are several steps that teachers can take to try to counteract this tendency.

- Have first-hand experience available as well as books.
- Provide several different books at various levels of difficulty and detail for each group.
- Encourage small groups of children to generate questions which they want to know the answers to.
- Show small groups how to use the contents, index and headings to scan for particular answers.
- Show small groups how to jot down key words and phrases and summarise passages in note form (noting the title and page number for future reference).
- Show small groups how to group information from various sources, using colours or numbers.
- Help them to create logical orders for their findings.
- Provide real audiences for the finished drafts or mini-lectures, to make all the effort worth while.

It was with these ideas in mind that we continued our consideration of pets in one class of nine-year-olds. We had started with stories from personal experience, first in the story-telling circle, and then written, illustrated and mounted in our class book. The children greatly enjoyed hearing their stories read aloud, and reading each other's. They were extremely keen to show their pets to each other so we arranged for a number of healthy creatures to be brought to school, in safe containers, on a particular day. (Teachers wishing to do something like this should check the regulations of their LEAs for hygiene and safety. Terrapins, in particular, can be a health hazard for people, and diseases can spread quickly among animals. It is also useful to have more than one adult available, for example, student teachers or parents.)

For each group of about four children there were reference books, paper for jottings, paper for sketching, and an animal and its owner. The school provided a duck, rabbit and gerbils; we also had a hooded rat, Siamese mice, a hamster, and some zebra finches. There was a good variety for comparison of tooth and claw, and thus living habits. We encouraged the owners to show their group how to handle their pets and to answer questions. We asked the children to jot down all the questions asked. Their brief was to prepare a talk-demonstration about their animal for the rest of the class. Answers to their questions were to come from their own observations, from the owner, or the monitor in the case of the school animals, and from the reference books. We expected to hear about two talk-demonstrations a week, after this initial exploration. Many of the children decided to write up their own individual commentaries on the animal they were studying to go into a sequel to the pets' story book.

Kirsty's notes show the process and her thinking very clearly. Unfortunately, her original scrawl and coloured underlining cannot be reproduced here. In this typed version, the underlinings are Kirsty's and represent answers to questions. The crossings out are also Kirsty's own. The underlined numbers represent Kirsty's different colours, where at the end of her note-taking it was suggested that she use colours to help her to categorise her material. Kirsty's chosen categories are shown in her plan, although we notice that in the plan and in her final draft, '4' is used for items to do with teeth, though in her notes, '4' is used for claws as well as teeth.

Kirsty, aged nine to ten

First draft – questions, notes

> Mice
> 1 **4** Claws are sharp
> 2 **4** They use then for picking up their food
> 3 **4** They are also sharp because they have to break open nuts and their other
> 4 food. I would like to find out some more about the mice.
> 5 **2** Do they get bigger or their tails? <u>Only a little bit.</u>
> 6 **2** How do you hold them? <u>By their tail.</u>
> 7 If they are in a hurry they jump very fast. <u>Frightened they jump</u>
> 8 <u>to get away.</u>
> 9 **3** They explore everywhere and when they find somewhere they make a house
> 10 out of the things they can find.

This first section of Kirsty's notes, seems to come directly from the oral observations and questions of her group, as they handle baby mice, discovering for themselves the sharpness of their claws, and listening to Philip's, the owner's, explanations about the claws and teeth. Kirsty writes 'I would like to find out some more about the mice.' (line 4) and she proceeds to do so. The question 'Do they get bigger or their tails?' (line 5) is ambiguous, and Kirsty's answer 'Only a little bit.' does not enlighten us, but the question does provide a focus for her searches in the reference books, as we see in her notes (lines 12, 15, and 17–18) in the next extract. By the final draft Kirsty seems to have resolved the problem to her own satisfaction (lines 39, 41).

a. Mice do get a little bit bigger (line 5).

b. Their tails do get bigger and they grow to about 12 cm (line 39).

c. A field mouse has a longer tail than a tame mouse (line 41).

> 11 *Field Mice*
> 12 /**2** I think on a field mouse the tail is longer. /**3** A pair of mice were
> 13 once known to have made their nest in a cigar box. /**3** Field mice are
> 14 becoming scarce and are only found in certain places. /**2** British
> 15 mice are the most common for the long tailed field mouse. /**1** If they are
> 16 wild they feed at night. /**3** The field mice would make their nests in and
> 17 around the corn field. ~~The sort we have today come from.~~ /**2** The tail
> 18 grows to about 12 cm. /**1** Mice do not eat cheese. /**1** They eat all sorts of
> 19 other things like corn, barley. That's what the field mice eat. The tame
> 20 ones eat bread in milk./

This section of her notes seems to stem partly from the reference books as at lines 12–14, 'A pair of mice were once *known to have made* their nest in a cigar box. Field mice are becoming scarce and *are only to be found* in certain places.'. Even if not directly copied, the sections in italics are based on the literary and formal style of the books. But alongside these sections we see the more colloquial and probably orally based 'I think on a field mouse the tail is longer.' (line 12) and 'They eat all sorts of other things like corn, barley. That's what the field mice eat. The tame ones eat bread in milk.' (lines 18–20).

Kirsty shows some awareness of these two different styles in the next part of her notes:

> 21 ~~The Mouse's Claws~~
> 22 ~~I am doing about Philip's mice. When the claws are very sharp and small they~~
> 23 ~~use them for all sorts.~~
> 24 /3 First the female mouse makes a nest. It does not take very long. They
> 25 make it by weaving in and out with straw and bits of wool in the middle for
> 26 the babies to lie on. /5 When they do have their babies they have five or
> 27 even more. They take about two weeks to open their eyes./

She starts her first draft very directly and colloquially with 'I am doing about Philip's mice. When the claws are very sharp . . .' (line 22) but then crosses out the heading and all the writing, and gathers some more fascinating information about how the female mouse builds her nest and about the babies. This probably comes partly from the books, partly from Philip and partly from observation. Indeed, the 'wool' (line 25), which might be sheep's wool, becomes cotton wool (line 46). This is caused either by ignorance, or, more likely, a conflation of the field mouse's nest with that of the tame mouse.

All the way through the notes, and in the final draft, we see Kirsty selecting what to include and what to leave out. In the notes, she crosses out 'the sort we have today come from' (line 17) as being inappropriate to her present concerns. As she chooses the headings under which she will try to group her material, she jots them down in the order in which they happen to occur to her:

> 28 *Plan*
> 29 1 – Food
> 30 2 – Tail
> 31 3 – Homes
> 32 4 – Teeth
> 33 5 – Babies

Her categories are all nouns, and this results in a different final draft from that which she would have produced if she had chosen verbs, or a series of questions, or given herself a chronological order based on the life-cycle of the mouse. Neither her headings, nor her ordering of them, seem incongruous to Kirsty at nine. On this occasion, she had already written her final draft, beautifully set out, and was well pleased with her efforts, before we returned to her. On a future occasion, we would hope to catch her at the planning stage, to help her to find a less arbitrary sequence. However, even with its shortcomings, Kirsty's final draft (page 43) is interesting. She manages to maintain a more impersonal, informative style, and incorporates a number of touches that show her confidently adopting the role of informer. We see this especially with 'They also enjoy it.' (line 50), and 'When they do get fur on, you may touch them.' (line 54), which represent new information, and where she tells her readers 'the proper way to hold it is by its tail.' (line 40).

The final draft also includes a number of transformations of the material in her notes. For example, 'If they are wild they feed at night.' (line 15), becomes 'If the mouse is wild it would feed at night-time.' (line 35). 'They explore everywhere and when they find somewhere they make a house out of the things they can find.' (line 9), becomes 'They explore every day looking for a home.' (line 43). The information 'They use their teeth to gnaw away at the wood which helps to make their homes' (line 48) is new and did not appear anywhere in the notes. On the other hand, some of the information in the notes is not included in the final draft, for example, lines 1 and 2, 21 and 22 about the mouse's claws.

It would seem then, that this way of working can help the more fluent writers to learn much more than the facts about the particular topic they are studying. Over the months and years, they will be learning the following skills.

Kirsty *Final draft*

Mice

Food

35 If the mouse is wild it would feed at night-time.
36 The field mouse eats things like corn and barley.
37 They do not eat cheese.

Tails

39 Their tails do get bigger and they grow to about twelve centimetres. If the
40 mouse bites and you are scared of it doing so. The proper way to hold it is
41 by its tail. A field mouse has a longer tail than a tame mouse.

Homes

43 They explore every day looking for a home. A pair of mice were once known
44 to have made their nest in a cigar box. Field mice make their homes in and
45 around a corn field. They make their nests by weaving in and out. They put
46 cotton wool in for the babies to lay on.

Teeth

48 They use their teeth to gnaw away at the wood which helps to make their
49 homes.
50 They also enjoy it.

Babies

52 When the mother has babies she has five or even more. It takes about eleven
53 days for them to open their eyes. If anybody touches them the mother will
54 eat the babies. When they do get fur on you may touch them.

- How to ask questions.
- How to search for answers from observations, experts and books.
- How to use reference books.
- How to take notes.
- How to impose order on such notes.
- How to draft, redraft and edit.
- How to present a final draft.
- How to respond to other people's work.

This seems to be much more worthwhile than the admittedly neater and probably better organised writing resulting from dictated or copied notes.

Building an imaginary world

A further form of support that is particularly enabling for children as writers and readers, is the creation of an imaginary world, building over several weeks, with the teacher, as well as the children, participating, often in role, in the gradual development of the story. Such gradual development can free the children to try out different kinds of writing, in context, that are less than a complete narrative in themselves. There might be little opportunity otherwise for children to experiment with elements of story writing, such as a dialogue or a monologue in role, or giving an individual's account of the setting or the social relationships of an imaginary time or place (including other historical or geographical settings). For the class as appreciative audience, each element may add to, or deepen, understanding of particular aspects of the created world. For the child, there is more likely to be room for human learning alongside language learning if the demands of structuring are reduced through working on one element at a time, instead of having to integrate several elements into a complex 'complete' story.

We see this dramatically revealed in John's decision in 'What would you be?'. It seems that posing himself a question, and attempting to answer it, has allowed John to create for himself a much more complicated structure than he would normally use in a story. We guess this was only possible because of the support of the extended work related to the book, and the immediately preceding role play. His main structure follows directly from his own title:

> What would you be?
>
> 1) I would be a monkey...
> 2) But if I were a monkey...
> 3) So I would be magic...

However, John does far more than simply set down alternatives:

John, aged ten   *First draft*

> I would like to be a monkey, because they could swing in the trees and be a messinjar. Because nowone would be-atle to catch me, and I would be very quickly. But if I were a monkey I would not be and (?) to tork English or the languig the faun sauk (?). So I would like to be majek Or be a yoman but majek, so I could chage into eny cand of animal of or thing.

He thinks each alternative over, arguing for and against each one as he goes along. The structural pattern he makes looks like this:

1 **Be** a monkey
    because they could swing in the trees
    because no one would be able to catch me
    because I would be very quick

    and (**thus**) could be a messenger
2 **But** I would not be able to talk English
                       or
3 **So be** magic
    or a human **but** magic
    so I could change into any kind of animal
                        or

Thus, as well as getting the central structure right, John gets each of the logical connectors (because, but, so and or) right too, apart from one tiny slip. He integrates them into one complete argument which is correct at the logical level, and maintains sufficient control to try out additional alternatives even at the end of his arguments 'be magic **or** be a human but magic ... any kind of animal **or** thing'.

A diagram will help us to *expose* for ourselves the scheme of thinking behind John's writing – the argument with its proposals, counter-proposals, alternatives, reasons and decisions.

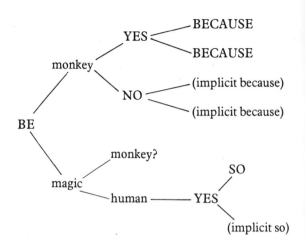

When we see John's reasoning set out step by step, we recognise how different it is to constructing a story based on a set of events arranged in correct time sequence. And when we remember that John, at ten years of age, is still struggling with many aspects of the written medium, his achievement is all the more commendable. In this case, further support from the teacher will take the form of open recognition of the successful thinking and the effort it involved. A teacher might also want to create the diagram from a pupil's writing in order to present visually to the pupil and some of his peers the quality of his thinking. This might be particularly useful with older writers where poor spelling and handwriting may undermine self confidence.

Diagrams to organise ideas

There are, however, occasions when diagrams can help the children to *organise* their thinking. In particular, tree diagrams, whether arranged horizontally, as in John's case, or vertically, can make clear the logical relations and connections required. A good time to use tree diagrams is when a class, small group or year group, is planning a project, in humanities or environmental studies perhaps. It is possible to collect randomly children's ideas for topics that individuals or small groups might study. Then the children can usually group ideas of similar status (using coloured chalks), spot omissions, and arrange the groups hierarchically. The Health Education project referred to earlier provided an opportunity for one class of nine-year-olds to work out together what they would like, and ought, to study under the headings 'How we explore our world' and 'How we look after our bodies'. Their completed diagram looked like this:

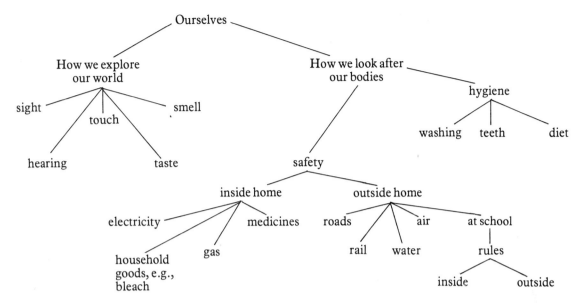

Clearly, each sub-category can be further sub-divided, but with a diagram it is easy to spot areas that have been given extensive treatment, and areas that have been neglected. For example, under 'safety in the home', 'heat' could be a superordinate:

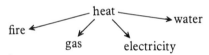

It is likely that many teachers use tree diagrams and flow diagrams when planning their schemes of work for the term and year. We feel that it is also important to share this technique with the children, so that they too can have access to a powerful tool which can lay bare logical relationships and choices.

One child, ten-year-old Jason, discovered for himself the benefit of using a flow diagram to depict a process. We found this in his notes.

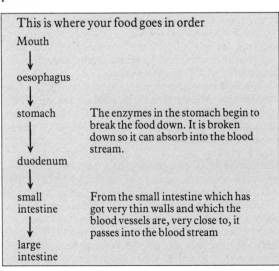

Thus he was able not only to keep the events in the process in order, but to include explanation and commentary about what happens to the food, alongside the sequence of where the food goes.

The advantage of using a flow diagram with a commentary alongside in this way only hit us when we found signs of struggle in his notes further down the page:

> How do we get the oxygen that burns up glucose for energy? For energy to be released we need oxygen. There is oxygen in the air. We take air into our body by breathing. We take good air into our lungs and we breathe out bad air which is air plus carbon dioxide and oxygen which passes into the blood stream to the part of the body where it is needed and there burns up the glucose into energy.

The three cues of his difficulty:

- the loss of meaning,
- the breakdown of sentence structure and
- the loss of punctuation,

all indicate that support is needed with the *thinking*, not merely correction of the writing. To find exactly what is the problem, we need to look at the process slowly, as Jason describes it (overleaf).

◀ *Jason, aged ten*

Process à la Jason	Commentary
1 We take good air into our lungs	
2 we breathe out bad air	which is air plus carbon dioxide
3 and oxygen	which passes into the blood stream to
4 the part of the body	where it is needed and there burns up the glucose into energy

The flow ought to be straightforward:

good air ⟶ lungs ⟶ blood stream ⟶ parts of body.

The problem is that the flow branches in the lungs, with used air coming out as well as good air coming in. Jason's implicit flow diagram hasn't allowed for this branching, so '2' interferes with the flow of '1', '3' and '4'. Also, the chunks of commentary he needs to fit in alongside the implicit flow diagram are probably too large to handle.

There are various ways in which the process with its branch could be diagrammed. One that we could use with Jason might look something like this:

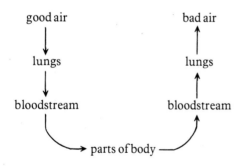

If we set it out carefully there will be space for commentary on both sides.

These are the benefits of diagramming a process in advance of elaborating the commentary:

1 It invites step by step progression.
2 Omissions or additional factors to be accommodated show up.
3 This simplifies the sentence structure that the commentary requires.
4 This, in turn, reduces the punctuation demands.

Since we first reported Jason's discovery, several other applications of flow diagram plus commentary depicting a process have turned up in science and in geography.

Summary

All of the structures considered in this chapter, whether implicit or explicit, have appeared in the writing of junior-age children. Sometimes, teachers will want to observe quietly, for they recognise that even the apparently simple request for an alternative phrase, to replace, for example, 'When I was born', may put additional burdens on a writer already struggling with surface features and the demands of writing for a new purpose or a new audience. On other occasions teachers will want to share a powerful tool such as diagramming to help children to plan their stories and projects. It seems that children also absorb much through their reading and through the literature we read to them.

Let us now give a summary of the structures considered here, in the form of a diagrammatic overview (page 47).

References

Applebee, A. N., *The Child's Concept of Story – Ages Two to Seventeen*, University of Chicago Press, 1978.
Barry, S., *Boffy and the Teacher Eater*, Armada Lions, London, 1971.
Britton, J., et al, *The Development of Writing Abilities (11–18)*, Macmillan, London, 1975.
Pradl, G. M., (ed), *Prospect and Retrospect: Selected Essays of James Britton*, Heinemann Educational Books, 1982.

Notes and acknowledgements

The material for this chapter has come from joint work with teachers in several schools and discussions with many groups of teachers and advisers, and my colleagues in the Bretton Hall College Language Development Unit (LDU), Angela Wilson and John Dixon, to whom I am particularly indebted. Joe Briel, Head of the Department of Professional and Human Studies, and the Bretton Hall Academic Board have made the LDU venture possible.

Special acknowledgement must be made to Maria Kojs of Crigglestone Middle School, Wakefield, for the 'Boffy' stories and 'Me as a Baby' writing, as well as the tree diagrams on 'Ourselves'. Colin Urch, the Wakefield English Adviser is thanked for his continued support. I am grateful to the teachers of Delf Hill Middle School, Bradford, particularly Joy Wood, Elaine Shack and Pat Richardson, who made possible the analysis of Julie's work on the buffalo, and Jason's flow chart of a process; to Jenny Leach, the Bradford English Adviser, and the Working Party of Bradford teachers who met regularly for three years and whose thinking and enthusiasm have supported the Bretton LDU. Further examples of their work can be seen in LDU Booklets One, A and B. Other adaptations of some of the

ORGANISING WRITING TOGETHER 47

Diagrammatic overview of some of the structures available to junior-age children considered in this chapter

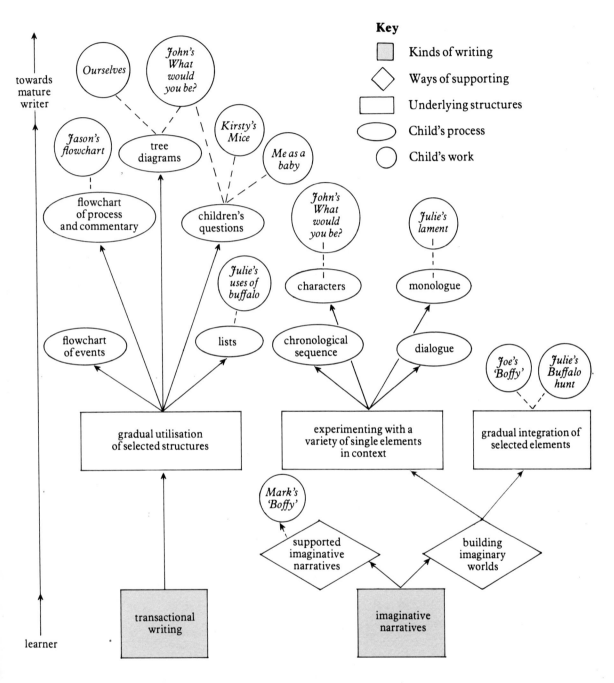

structuring ideas can be found in the forthcoming LDU booklet *One Way of Working* featuring the Driffield Pyramid Group, encouraged by the Humberside English Adviser, Derek Fulford. Margaret Smith, Jane Waterhouse, Ann Goodall and Judith Grace, teachers in the first year team of Scissett Middle School, Kirklees, participated in the joint experiment of building an imaginary world. I am grateful to them and to Tony Barringer, the Kirklees English Adviser.

Examples of this approach may be seen in LDU Booklet Two and the LDU booklets by Angela Wilson, on fiction and role play as starting points for writing.

It is interesting to note that 'What would you be?' can fall equally appropriately on the 'Transactional' or the 'Imaginative' side of the diagram above, and often writing that falls into each of these categories will be produced.

Beyond Babel: linguistic diversity and children's writing
Viv Edwards

What are the implications of linguistic diversity for children's writing? For most teachers this question can be restated in the form of 'What do I do when children use a dialect form or make a second language learning error in their writing?' We shall consider this question separately for dialect-speaking and bilingual children, though a number of similarities between these two groups will emerge.

Dialect forms in writing

Given that educational success and social mobility depend on a child's ability to use standard English, it is perhaps not surprising that many teachers react adversely to dialect forms in children's writing. However, this issue needs to be seen in perspective. Although departures from standard English such as 'we was' and 'I seen' are subjected to strong criticism, the number of such differences between the standard and other dialects of English is, in fact, relatively small. Very young children, for the most part, produce short stretches of writing which will frequently contain no dialect features at all. Examples such as 'done' in the story by Sarah below form only a tiny proportion of young children's actual writing.

Many teachers feel that it is in the children's best interest that dialect features such as these should be drawn to their attention even at this early stage. However, it is possible to argue that intervention of this kind is unwarranted. At a time when the physical and mental effort required of young children in putting pen to paper is so great, attempts to persuade them that a form used regularly in their community is unacceptable are likely to be confusing and will hardly enhance either pleasure or a feeling of achievement in the writing process. The course which Sarah's teacher has chosen is likely to be a good deal more productive. By entering into a dialogue and responding to the child's 'story' with some information about herself, she is helping to foster the idea of writing as a communicative act, and to develop Sarah's sense of herself as a writer. She also, incidentally, provides her with a model of the standard form 'did'. There is a

marked difference between this kind of approach and one which insists that the dialect form is 'wrong' and the standard variant is 'right'.

As children's writing develops other questions of 'correctness' present themselves. Non-standard features do appear with greater frequency, but it is still important to view the incidence of dialect forms in the total context of the child's progress as a writer. Take, for instance, the piece of writing by nine-year-old Wayne shown below.

Given Wayne's stage of development as a novice writer, there are some obvious inaccuracies in his piece. These include fifteen words mis-spelled, nineteen mistakes in punctuation, he omits a word ('play the park'), and uses one wrong connective ('so was my brother'). In contrast, non-standard English features appear just three times: 'we was hungry', 'we seen drackysler' and 'nobody seen my brother'. If a child writes fluently and has no problem with spelling and punctuation but still uses dialect forms, then there would certainly be a case for discussing the question of 'appropriateness', and the need for standard rather than dialect forms in situations such as formal writing. However, where children like Wayne are still grappling with the technical aspects of transcription and composition, it is reasonable that the presence of dialect features should come low on the teacher's list of priorities and not be allowed to assume exaggerated importance.

Many people, even when presented with arguments such as those outlined above, still feel that they have a moral duty to 'correct' dialect forms in children's writing. However, such corrections are very often inconsistent and confusing. Take, for instance, the teacher-response to a piece of work produced by a ten-year-old black British child who was still showing features of West Indian Creole in her writing (page 50).

In walse me my dad and my
mum and my brothers and sisters
went to a fair. It was 1981 when
we went. we set off in the
morning. We went in a coach
It took us three hours to
get there. It was fun there
It was eight o'clock when we
reached there. It was eleven oclock
when we got out of the coach
we went streght into the
fair. we was hungry so we had
our diner we had salad I wasnot
very hungry so was my brother.
so my dad said go and play the
the park so we did. we went on
the gost train. Me and my brother
fell off the gost train it was
skery in there. we seen drackysler.
my mum and my dad had finished
theyer diner and then they packed
away and my mum said where is wayne
my dad said they are in the
park so they went into the park
and nobody seen my Brother

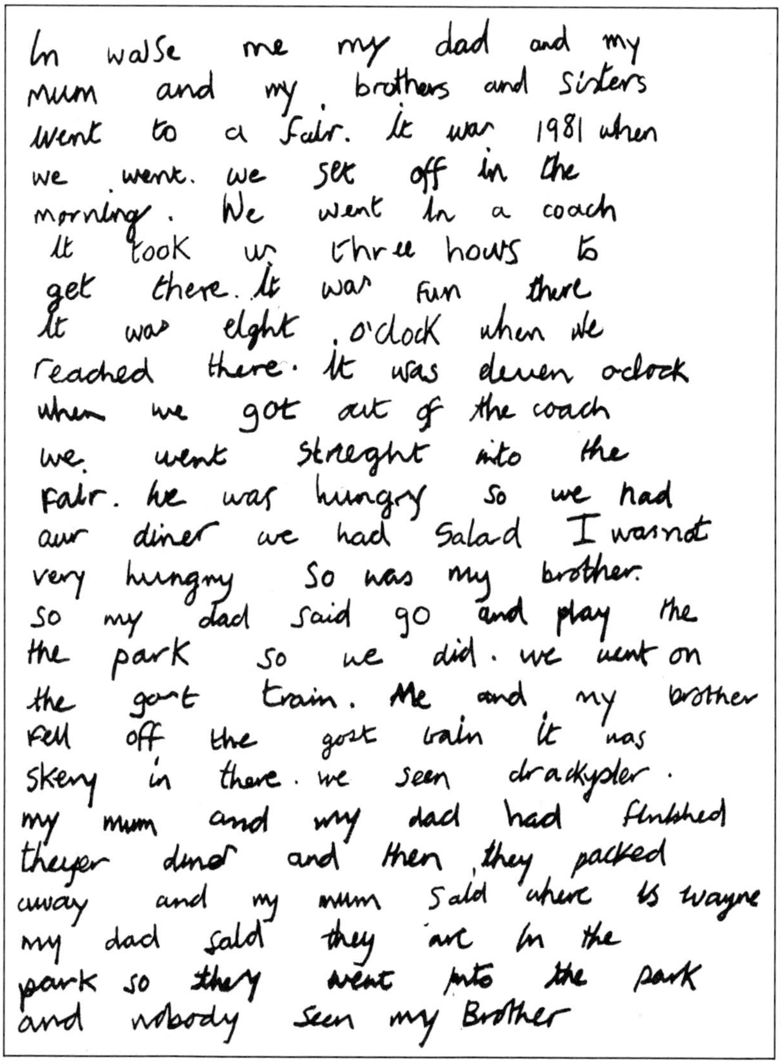

It look very good

It smell cremmy

It's very smooth texture

It's very brown

It stand like a stone

It smell like milk

ABDUL

I am wiating about my tarin sat
I have a toy tarin it go's on a ryyl. it
go's very fast. it go's on elactarc and
it his batans and the butans can
be control. olso you can control the
tarin in any deracsan and olso
you can put wood on top off the
roof and it has a cemaney where
the samke coms out. and runod
the tarin there are plastc trees
and plaste sattysun. dat all it has
on my toy

The only correction which the teacher made to this piece of writing was to the second line where 'smell' was changed to 'smells'. However, it is difficult to imagine what conclusions the child is supposed to draw when no changes are made to 'look' (line 1), to 'stand' (line 5), or indeed to 'smell' when it reappears in the last line. The teacher has clearly chosen not to change all the non-standard forms knowing that the child would find it demoralizing to find her work covered with red pen marks. Such a course, if rigorously pursued, would also be extremely time-consuming. However, the consequence of *ad hoc* correction strategies will most likely be confusion, in which case the only thing achieved by such a course will be a lightening of the teacher's conscience.

As children's writing develops there will be many opportunities to discuss the question of the appropriateness of dialect and standard forms for different situations. Indeed, on some occasions, children themselves will initiate such discussion. This is therefore not an area which lends itself to easy solutions. It is both impractical and imprudent to insist that dialect features in children's writing should always be corrected. But, by the same token, it is short-sighted to suggest that children's attention should never be drawn to dialect difference. The individual child's particular needs and stage of development should be carefully assessed before deciding on the appropriate course of action. Questions which the teacher might ask in deciding upon the most helpful course of action will include these:

- Is the child's writing fluent and imaginative?
- Are the child's transcription skills, i.e., spelling, punctuation and general organisation of written work, satisfactory?
- Does the child have the opportunity to use and hear different kinds of language in the wide range of situations which can be created using puppets, role play, drama and story telling?

If the answers to all of these questions are 'yes', the child is likely to be both ready and receptive to discussions of appropriateness of dialect forms in writing. However, if any of the questions should produce a 'no', teacher-efforts to encourage standard forms are almost certainly doomed to failure.

Second language errors in children's writing

The same global approach is both helpful and necessary in dealing with second language learning errors in children's writing. All too often it is possible to exaggerate the nature and extent of a problem. Take, for instance, ten-year-old Abdul's description of his train set (above), written when he had been in England for one year.

A first reaction to this piece of writing might well be that Abdul's language learning problems are so great that it would be difficult for a non-specialist teacher to know where to start. Yet a closer look reveals some very interesting patterns:

- Like many native speakers of his age, he shows a monotonous use of 'and' for joining sentences and does not attempt any kind of subordination.
- He does, however, have a clear idea of sentences and marks them off with a full stop in every case but one.
- Most of the other technical difficulties relate to spelling mistakes. 'Wiating', 'go's', 'his', 'olso', 'off' and 'coms' are almost certainly mis-spellings.
- Various other words, in contrast, give interesting indications of the sound pattern of his mother tongue. The insertion of a vowel between two

consonants in 'tarin', 'elactarc', 'samke' and 'sattysun' would suggest that certain combinations are not permissible in his language. The use of 'a' in 'sat', 'elactarc', 'batans' and 'deracsan' would suggest that his vowel system does not coincide with that of English and that the 'a' vowel has a wider distribution in Punjabi. This is in fact the case on both counts. When seen in this light Abdul is clearly not a wild and hopeless guesser, but is applying himself intelligently to the task of spelling English words.

- Just as significant, there are only two mistakes ('can be control' and 'dat all it has') which could be explained in terms of second language learning errors.

The most reasonable conclusion is that Abdul is a child who is making considerable progress and is showing a constructive and intelligent approach to the learning of another language.

The question remains as to what form teacher-intervention, if any, should take. Teachers should try to base their decisions on a close examination of a wide range of children's writing rather than on isolated examples as it is very easy to identify a form as a second language learning problem when it is, quite simply, a slip or omission of the same kind that native speakers make.

Nine-year-old Marco, for instance, writes about his cousin as follows:

> My cousin live in Italy. She has long hair and brown eye. She has nine years old. Her father has a shop at Monserrato. The garden isn't big.

Marco makes three mistakes in this piece of writing.
- He omits the 's' in 'lives'.
- He uses singular 'eye' and not 'eyes'.
- He puts 'has' and not 'is nine years old'.

The last mistake can be traced to an idiom found in Italian and various other European languages, and it might well be a good idea for the teacher to draw his attention to this point of difference. It is not possible, however, to say with any degree of confidence on the basis of this short stretch of writing whether or not Marco has general problems with plurals and third person singular present tense forms. We therefore need to consider other examples of his work and find, in fact, that he uses plurals without any difficulty (thus the use of 'eye' for 'eyes' is almost certainly a slip), but that third person singular present tense forms are more problematic, as this example shows:

> Its the birthday of Fudge, he invite a lot of friends. One of them give him a book but Fudge don't like the present and he throw it across the room. then they jump around the room. the naibor dauhters climb up, she was wary angri so the mather of Fudge say to her to bring a pice of cake and so she did. Then Fudge and his friends jump in the new bed, the mather of Fudge yell: "don't jump in the new bed!" Fudge say: "New bed greet boy!"

In responding to a bilingual child's writing, it is important to bear in mind the actual strategies which we use in learning another language. Rather than simply proceeding from an incorrect to the correct form, we progress through a series of steps, each approximating more closely to the target language. Very often the class teacher's most important role is to provide the child with real opportunities for communication, both with the teacher and with other children, since it is only in this way that they can formulate rules as to how the language works and then put these rules to the test. In the speech situation, teacher correction is likely to be perceived as a nuisance by the child, whose main objective is the communication of information rather than grammatical accuracy. In the more studied act of writing, however, teacher intervention can be a good deal more productive. Where a mistake is made often and consistently, as in the case of third person singular present tense forms in Marco's writing, it is worth drawing the child's attention to it, wherever possible providing practice, perhaps in the form of a game. It is obviously important to concentrate on one small area at a time if you are to avoid continually confusing the child, and this is a fruitful area for co-operation between the class teacher and any specialist support staff in the school.

Opportunities for writing in other dialects and languages

Very often teachers speak only one language fluently. Often they work in areas geographically remote from where they spent their own childhood and are therefore unsure about the exact pronunciation of words or how sentences are formed in the dialect spoken where they now live. It is often a sense of personal insecurity that makes them shy away from allowing children to write in their own language or dialect. In so doing, however, they are missing out on valuable opportunities which allow children to develop a sense of themselves as writers, perhaps the most important factor in producing fluent and competent writing.

If we look first at the question of dialect writing there is admittedly a dearth of suitable published material which can provide a model or stimulus for children's writing. Yet a little diligence will often produce interesting results. Lancashire dialect is to be found in books like M. Edgar's *The Lion and Albert*, Scots dialect in D. C. Thomson's *The Broons* and *Oor Wullie* and Cockney in J. Lawrence's *Rabbit and Pork, Rhyming Talk*; traditional Eli and Enoch stories abound in Black Country publications. Occasional dialect poems or short stories can also be found in anthologies as readily available as G. Summerfield's *Voices*. Various community publishing projects like Centerprise, the Black Ink Collective and the Peckham Publishing Project have produced short stories and biographies in British and Caribbean dialects, many of which can be adapted for or used directly with young children. The ILEA English Centre is another valuable source of dialect writing. There are also many opportunities for children to produce their own materials, drawing on parents, grandparents and their own experience. Dialect can be used in a wide range of writing to create humour, pathos, immediacy and vitality. Take this account of her new neighbours written by Jennifer, the British-born daughter of Barbadian parents:

Writing by children in other languages can also be used to considerable effect. *Redlands Magazine*, produced by Redlands Primary School in Reading, is an excellent example of interesting and varied writing by young children. Alongside the stories, jokes, poems, book reviews, recipes and tongue twisters in English are contributions in several other languages. Lorna, for instance, writes about her house in Venezuela (see page 53).

The inclusion of examples such as this can achieve a number of ends. It demonstrates that languages other than English are both respected and valued by the school. If children are in the process of learning English, it gives them the opportunity to demonstrate that, although they may not yet be able to perform on a level with native speakers, they are equally competent in their mother tongue. If children are already bilingual, it allows them to show their friends and peers skills which play an important part in their family lives. Bilingualism is thus presented as something positive, and not as a problem or an obstacle to learning English. Nor should the question of bilingual children's writing be polarised in terms of either English or the mother tongue, since there are

> It was Saturday morning and Hilda come and knock on our front door.
> "Morning Mrs Small," she said.
> "Morning Hilda," said my mum.
> "Anyway, I see you've got some snobby neighbours next door."
> "How do you know?" said my mum.
> "Oh, I just been looking through my curtains," said Hilda.
> "You always looking through your curtains," said my mum.
> "Anyway, they still out there?" said my mum.
> "Oh yes," said Hilda.
> We went outside to meet our snobby neighbours.
> "Oh, mind my furniture!" said the woman.
> "Mind my goldfish!" said the man.
> "Mummy, Mummy, Mummy, that boy pull my pony tail!"
> "Naughty little boy!..... I told you let's go to America. But no, you insist let's go to Reading. 'Nice people there," you said.
> "Nice fashion people. Oh, they so lovely!' But now we surrounded by this scruffy lot and unkind."
> "How dare you call us scruffy lot! We nice people round here.
> Who you talking about? You the unkind and scruffy lot. You come round here making trouble about our street."
> "Alfred, do something!"
> "Yes, don't insult my wife!"
> "Is that all you have to say? Is that all you have to say?"
> "Now, I'm going. I'm not standing here to be insulted by this woman. Come on Sally, let's go."
> Me and my mum and Sally went inside and we laughed about that the whole day.

> Mi casa en Maturin
>
> Yo me llama Lorna. Cuando yo vivia en Venezuela mi casa era bonita y grande. En mi vivian mi abuela y mi hermana, mama y papas, en la mañana cuando yo me levantaba iva para la esebela. A las 8.00 de la mañana yo asia bastante trabajo en mi colegio, despues me iva para mi casa y me tomaba mi almuerzo y despues me ponia hacer mis tareas de la escuela.
>
> Lorna Manzi

often opportunities for using both languages and developing children's translation skills in the process. Zebin, for instance, became involved in discussions about snakes with other Punjabi-speaking children in his class. It was only natural that experiences which had taken place in Pakistan should be recounted first in Punjabi, and his teacher, Audrey Gregory, took advantage of the excitement generated by the initial story-telling to encourage Zebin and his friends to write down these stories first in Urdu, the literary language used by Pakistanis, and then in English (see page 54).

Conclusion

Two broad approaches to linguistic diversity can be discerned in British education. The first, more traditional, approach sees diversity as a problem. The second approach regards linguistic diversity as a resource. Instead of treating children as *tabulae rasae*, and making no reference to the considerable language skills which they bring with them to the classroom, every attempt is made to build upon existing knowledge to broaden their linguistic repertoires. The teacher's task is still to teach standard English, but this aim is felt to be more readily achieved by accepting and valuing children's existing language skills than by criticising or ignoring them.

> ایک سانپ ایک مرغی مود میں جھپٹ گیا
>
> [Urdu handwritten text]
>
> ختم شد

one day I was helping my
grand father to kill a chicken
My grand father saw a snake
hiding in the field ~~Then~~ the
snake escaped He ran away
to his hole in a tree Then my grand father was
scared The chicken was bloody but we didn't
let go of it we killd It in my family not everybody
can kill a chicken ~~We~~ give the chicken to my
grand father and then he kills the chicken for
my family Then the snake wriggled away I don't
like snakes.

References

Books

Edgar, M., *The Lion and Albert*, Methuen, London, 1978.

Lawrence, J., *Rabbit and Pork, Rhyming Talk*, Hamish Hamilton, London, 1975.

Summerfield, G., *Voices*, Penguin Books, Harmondsworth, 1968.

Thomson, D. C., *Oor Wullie*, Thomson & Co, Glasgow, 1970.

Thomson, D. C., *The Broons*, Thomson & Co, Glasgow, 1971.

Community Publishing Projects

Black Ink Collective, 1 Gresham Road, London SW9.
Centerprise, 136 Kingsland High Street, London E8.
The English Centre, Ebury Teachers' Centre, Sutherland Street, London SW1.
Peckham Publishing Project, The Bookplace, 13 Peckham High Street, London SE15.

I would like to thank the children of Redlands and Katesgrove County Primary Schools, Reading, for letting me look at their work, and their teachers, Angela Redfern, Audrey Gregory and Liz Pye, for supplying examples of writing and for much valuable discussion.

Purposeful writing
Margaret Peters

Motivation to write

As adults we do not write unless we are strongly motivated to write. We write because we are moved to write and this 'being moved' highlights the other side of the motivational coin which is feeling. We write because we feel strongly about something. We write because we must, yet we expect children to write in school knowing full well that many do not feel strongly about what we expect them to write. We demand written news, the writing of diaries, even stories and poetry, and what do we get?

Diaries – I went to Star Wars.
           I have got a new space invader.
Stories – Once upon a time there was a giant.
Poetry – Often written as prose and punctuated into lines, each beginning with a capital letter, by the teacher and copied as 'poetry' by the child.

The stimulus for all this is from *outside* the child. There is no question that motivation to write must come from *within*, from a felt need to write. This is not to say that teachers are unaware of the value of purposeful writing. They hope they are exacting this by use of these means.

- Interest cards
- Resource Centre access
- Record keeping
- Nature diaries
- Sports reports
- Review of books – ostensibly for other children with a view to helping their selection of what to read

These may be purposeful, but they are teacher-imposed.

Relevant (guinea-pig) writing in school

As Hoffman (1976) describes so engagingly, some of the most pertinent writing activities that children pursue in school concern the care of pets. It was a Cheshire guinea-pig that inspired Johnson, referred to by Hoffman, to coin the now familiar phrase 'guinea-pig activity' – meaning relevant need to read and write. For Hoffman, this includes pet care, menu-writing, instructions on how to use equipment and, we can add, the quite rapturous delight in the circumstances surrounding the Christening of a teacher's baby at Dymchurch School. She speculates on that writing which emanates from children's felt need to write something in order to get something they cannot get through speech. It is only in such highly motivated writing that the spotlight is on the child with all the urgency of feeling that impels writing because there is no other way of getting the message across.

Legibility

Because writers make strong verbal demands they will write simply and explicitly. A writer must not create confusion in the mind of the reader or risk a wrong interpretation. Therefore handwriting is made legible. It is important, for instance, that a message to one's mother should be read correctly as 'Do not touch'.

Correctness or near-correctness of spelling to avoid distraction

Highly motivated activity demands, in itself, standards of precision, and one area of precision is spelling. If a message is to be communicated adequately it must be spelled with some accuracy, since, if it is inaccurate,

- the message might not get across,
- the one who receives the message will attend, not to the message, but to the wrongly spelt words.

For all of us, mis-spelt words hit us as we read since we all have within us, deeply embedded, the internalised model of the spelling system that makes us 'home in' on spelling errors and momentarily forget what the message is all about.

Examples of urgent writing

Here is a note written by a boy of ten where urgency demands as much precision as he can muster. It is crucial for him that his mother gets the facts right.

> Fech Juliann
> Juliann Richard
> & Gary b...
> because they
> mist bus.

Such writing is legible and written with decipherable spelling, otherwise the message would not be transmittable. Thus the child sees legibility and good spelling to be necessary to purposeful writing.

Urgency demands accuracy

Now an odd thing happens when a child or adult writes because they must, that is, when they write purposefully. In the first place, in urgent writing, we do not have to iron out the differences that occur in living speech. The writing is terse, laconic and clear, for example, ('Fech Juliann...'). What is more interesting is that urgent, purposeful writing is not only legible but tends to be spelt better than is customary for that particular child or adult. This is surprising in that the message is, by definition, 'urgent'. However, the need for the message to get across demands care in writing and an attempt at precision in spelling. And this is *self-imposed*. Individuals write carefully because they want the message to get across correctly.

This is increasingly recognised to be the case in writing in school. Many teachers have discovered that children write much better when they write for each other. They are anxious to write legibly and spell correctly as well as write within the idiom and the interests of the younger child. The increased awareness of another child that this entails, sharpens young writers' perceptions and increases their tendency to see the world from another person's point of view – a worthwhile activity if ever there was one.

Such writing for another child is teacher-imposed and not in any sense 'urgent' but it is valuable because the child is writing for an 'audience' other than the 'same old teacher' and it is therefore subject to the same self-imposed disciplines of legibility and accuracy, as 'urgent' message writing.

Constraints in non-purposeful (teacher-imposed) writing

Genuinely 'urgent' writing occurs when the writer is not in a position to communicate in speech because the intended reader is absent. It is not subject to the constraints enumerated and explored by so many who write about children's writing. Such writers set out to list the enormous differences between speech and writing – Rosen (1973), for example, contrasts 'speech' which is *fast* and *solitary* with writing which is *slow*, can be reshaped and worked on, and is *effortful*. There is, in writing, he says, more opportunity to sort out and organise their experiences for there is no face-to-face interaction.

Here again we have to distinguish between personal, urgent, purposeful writing and teacher-imposed writing, for the characteristics of purposeful writing are much more those of *speech* than of *writing*. Urgent, purposeful writing is, like speech, fast and solitary. It cannot be slow and effortful, and it is only reshaped in order to improve legibility and accuracy. So what is said of *speech* as opposed to *writing* can well be said of *purposeful writing* as opposed to *teacher-imposed* writing.

Again, the writer, we are told, gets no immediate linguistic or visual feedback telling whether the communication efforts are successful as is the case in speech. Nor does the purposeful writer. But it is not linguistic feedback which is necessary, but *action*. The feedback is in the functional outcome, the practical results. Purposeful writing is urgent writing. It is fast. It does not need to be worked on and reshaped. It is solitary and, like regulatory speech, it provokes action.

Self-imposed re-writing

It is those teachers who watch for the relevant moment who can exploit the possibilities of purposeful writing without imposing it. Hoffman (1976) presents examples of relevance, for this is her theme. What she does not note is the carefulness in handwriting, spelling and syntax that seems to be characteristic of such relevant writing. This is probably because much of the writing she discusses has been re-written. It is not, in fact, first draft. The child may be re-writing at the suggestion of a teacher for class instructions (in the care of pets), for wall display, for books for other children to read, etc.

It is only if the re-writing is self-imposed that the child will attend to handwriting and spelling for the right reasons, namely to force an audience to attend to the content by avoiding potential distractions of illegibility and bizarre spelling. A splendid example of self-imposed re-writing was told to the late Dr Elsa

> Harlow
> 1st march
> Dear Brigid Smith we all know that you are a rubbish rubbish driver and you should have your licence taken away years ago every one says so In remedial you should take driving lessons agane anyway thank you for takng us on the trip we all enjoyed it very much exept steven I liked elvis king of rock
> Thank you

Walters from the strange days of evacuation during the war. The story is told of a small gifted boy whose writing was 'like the trail of a spider crawling through the ink'. He was out in the snow, where the boys had built a fort. There were two sides defending and attacking, but neither side would let him join in. His teacher, to whom he appealed, suggested he should be the war correspondent. This meant he had to watch and write about what he saw. And he did, but then he spent the whole afternoon writing his report out *carefully*, legibly and with correct spelling. This was purposeful writing if ever there was.

'Remedial thirteen-year-old'

The letter shown above was received by a teacher after she had crashed the mini-bus in which she had taken her secondary remedial class out for the day.

Comparison with the following excerpt from the same boy's school 'writing book' at the same time, demonstrates the point I am making, that purposeful self-imposed writing makes a demand on the writer for careful writing, spelling and syntax. The writing of this letter flows along smoothly. It is legible and there are only two spelling mistakes 'agane' for 'again' and 'exept' for 'except' and these, as 'fech' and 'mist' in the example on page 56, are 'good errors' (Peters, 1985).

> A bicycle ride
> one day I went to call for my gang on my bike Jim, Ted hew was always hungry, bill and frank but my bike was all rusty and the where all still and there was a nother gang with biger lads hew had skooters and they full arownd on them and the leader was michael haves and he came rite into me and brock my bick wick made me really mad so I went and told my dad and mister billy our next dore naber took my dad round to michaels dad so michael had to by me another one wich made me very hurry and when I got it I went for a picknick with my gang and we went along the the country side we stoped ted from eating his sandwiches till we found the rite spot and on the way bills chane kept ecoming off so that made him slow but we did not care and then we came to a hill side and I tride to ride up it but I could not make it so I pulled my brake but I suded down agane and knocked all of them off there bikes and it was a long way down so we rode round it and we

We can see the self-imposed correction of 'rubbish' which, presumably for this thirteen-year-old, did not 'look right'! There is no punctuation, of course, but there is a move towards it in the thinking behind the writing, that is not in evidence in the boy's school exercise book.

Six-year-old and the supernatural

Another example is 'Dear teeth angels' found under the pillow of a six-year-old:

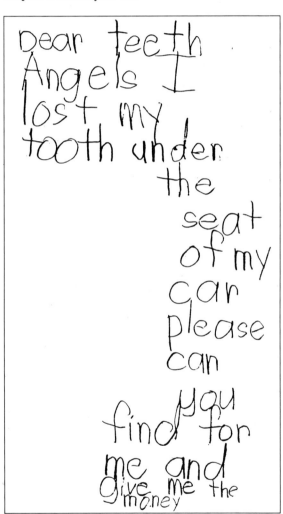

Now such a letter could easily have been intended for the parent to find, as, of course, are many letters to Father Christmas! This does not matter. Either the child is writing to a 'supernatural' power – in which case he really must be extra careful – or he is writing for the parents and they need to be propitiated into munificence! If the child is not sure and wants to hedge his bets he is going to be extra careful. 'Dear teeth angels' is written correctly and with style – unlike the boy's written work at school at about the same time:

Six-year-old's letter

On pages 59 to 62 is a letter written by a six-year-old to her 'dear uncle'. There is no question that a piece of writing such as this is written with 'loving care' and an incredible standard of legibility and precision, and for this reason it is presented in full. It is an example of a precise, articulate child from a highly educated Indian family, strangely introspective and with an unusual indication of an ability to see the world from another person's point of view. Such writing is unusual but it happens.

7th June 76

My so very dearly dear Uncle,

I bet this letter is going to meet you with quite a surprise when you find out who it is from. I shouldn't really reveal my name and better leave it to you to guess who I am. I can not make up my mind whether I should or whether I shouldn't tell you my name. Never mind, I have decided not to keep you in any more suspense any longer. Here I am right out with my name, Bhavani. I do hope that you have not forgot me. I say so because we have not met each other for quite a long time.

Uncle, I am not too well today. I have got some coil that I caught from Alika the other day. Hers went better and mine went worse. So she is off to school while I am off it. I was getting fed up and decided to do a letter to you. I miss you a lot because you are a very very nice uncle. I know I am very shy in front of you but I am getting over it slowly but surely. I hope you won't find me as shy as you did last time.

Uncle, I have turned out to be a left hander after all which I believe is pretty unusual for a Indian girl. But I'm sorry I just couldn't help. My mummy and daddy tried very hard to stop me from using my left hand for writing and eating. I try quite a lot still to see if I can ever get used to my right hand and give my parents and my sister a pleasant surprise. But I don't think I can win. I'll keep trying though.

Uncle, I'll be 7 next October. You will be glad to read that I have already finished about 20 books in reading at school. When we were in Rainhill, I was always ahead of everybody in the class. I always loved to go to school there because it was such a lovely school. But this new school that I have now gone to is not a good one. It gives me tummy ache when I think of it. Phaps that is why I don't keep well. I miss my old friend Johanne in the other school who was always so good to me. My daddy already knows that I don't like going to this new school very much. So he is sending me to a public school as soon as I get a seat there. I hope I should be O.K. then my daddy is awfully nice to me and never shouts at me.

Uncle, I don't really like our new house but it's quite big and roomy. My daddy has spent an awful lot of money on it. He has made it look quite nice really. We have got central heating put in and carpets all over. I am sure you will like it when you come over to see us. It's a very long time since you have been here last. It seems ages, it really does.

Uncle, I love to go on and on and hate to finish. But I'm afraid I have got to do so because there is no more lines left. And also I'm getting late for my dinner. My daddy is in the kitchen and he's shouting like mad. I will write a lot lot more next time. Please do ignore my mistakes. Bhavana

Eight-year-old – when strong feeling emerges!

Here is an example of an eight-year-old writing in school:

> Cruulty of aimmol
> The tiger is nell a exnt aimma tigers live in India and other parts of Asia, beve the hunts shot the tiger for / they skinn to yous has rugs. Wiy Do they have to cil tiger they have not Don eneth.

He has withdrawn to the Resource Centre and he starts copying, as is the unfortunate habit of so many children when making reference to other material. He copies the information presented about tigers – not correctly – for he is *copying* not only word by word but letter by letter, and it is neither meaningful reading nor meaningful writing, but *then* he sees his teacher hovering, and he knows 'she has a thing about not copying'. He has taken in the word 'tiger' – so he starts to write – from free association – and what he writes is well-structured and legible. What is more important is that this purposeful writing is spelt with more reasonable alternatives than when he was copying letter by letter.

Unreasonable spellings

> nell
> exnt
> aimma
> beve

Reasonable phonic alternatives
(good spelling errors)

> they skinn   cil
> yous   don
> has

Problems in writing down telephone messages

To support the argument that purposeful writing is of necessity careful writing, you will see below an urgent phone message taken by a doctor's seven-year-old daughter. It is legible and the spelling is adequate enough for the reader to receive the message correctly.

This message indicates the difficulty we have in taking messages aurally. There are no visual supports. It is interesting to note that the name was unfamiliar. She could not reconstitute the surname – and so wrote 'somebody or uther'. It is interesting to note that when children are dissatisfied with the spelling, they look at what they have written, cross it out and in all the cases quoted, got it right immediately. This is automatic self-correction, an invaluable self-imposed strategy, and something the teacher should consciously and deliberately reinforce.

> Kafe Some body or uther rug up to say that yoruer pashent who's bludpresn droped and he or her might have had a hart acc. And plese cod you contact her Kate somebody or uther
> Derrec will ring up later

Enhancement of style in purposeful writing

It is not only handwriting and spelling that are enhanced then, but style. These six-year-olds write in complex syntax: 'after you have finished on the phone', and 'because I woke up and I wanted to know what the time was'.

> Dear mummy.
> please don't forget
> to do my clock because
> I woke up and i wanted to
> know what the time was
>
> PS I waant
> mummy to tuck
> me in.

> daddy
> my bed
> is all rampled
> and I dont
> like please
> will you
> come and
> tuk me up
> aften you
> have finshe
> on the phone?

And contemplate this sad little note from a nine-year-old boy to his father – 'Fancy that', he writes, 'needles of all things'. By no means typical of a nine-year-old's school writing!

> Dad I am not
> going to go to
> school because paul
> David are saying
> that I have nicked som
> nedles fance that
> nedles of all things
> love Derek

Caught or taught?

Some of the examples used in this chapter are from children who have 'caught' spelling. Some, like the thirteen-year-old in the remedial class, have clearly been taught spelling. They are all exploiting their new-found medium in order to regulate others. Unless they are 'taught' what they have not 'caught' they cannot propitiate teeth angels, test fantasies, sustain a correspondence, amuse and gratify teachers, or regulate either their parents or themselves.

It is of the greatest importance, then, that children should be equipped with well-formed handwriting and safe learning-to-spell strategies to write purposefully. They are then free to write whatever they want, knowing that whoever reads what they have written will attend to the content not the spelling, the message not the medium.

Although much of this discussion has been concerned with spelling it cannot be stated too strongly that spelling is merely a sub-skill of writing, an activity that is only rarely pursued by adults and then only when it is purposeful and highly motivated. It has been shown that in children it occurs more spontaneously, but, again, only when they feel strongly about something and are hence highly motivated to write. That this purposeful writing occurs mostly at home and rarely at school, must concern teachers, for teachers expect, if not demand, that children write for a considerable part of their school life. Traditionally, and to this end there is much teaching of spelling, probably from lists, and such teaching does not necessarily produce purposeful writing. Although purpose in writing depends upon an inner urgency to commit a thought or an event to paper there is no question that communication is facilitated by control over the medium. In fact, what teachers demand is often very remote from purposeful writing.

There is a world of feeling between the six-year-old's teacher-imposed 'creative writing', 'If I were a millionaire' and the six-year-old's clandestine 'love letter' to his six-year-old friend. Much could be said about the teacher-imposed topic 'If I were a millionaire'. It is couched in unfamiliar syntax, but it is a doubtful moral situation in which to put a young child. In the same class the younger (less able?) children were told to write 'If I had a lot of money'. The materialism here assumed is inappropriate developmentally, ethically and motivationally. Furthermore, it is not in any sense urgent writing. Yet this is happening, in school today, and we read this from the exercise book of a six-year-old:

> If I was a millionaire I would build a house of bricks. I would buy a lot of books. I would buy a swimming pool and a bookshelf for all my books.

It is a far cry from the following which was part of a silent, written conversation between two six-year-olds and was prefaced by the three notes at the top of the next page.

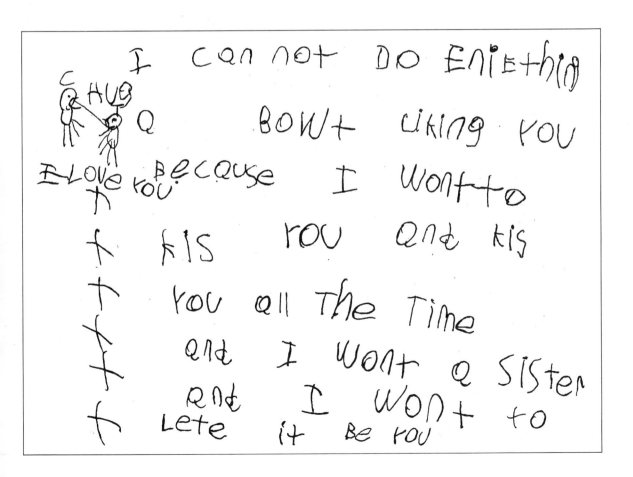

> From Timothy to Caroline – I luve you I am going to kiss you x x x

> From Caroline to Timothy – I love you and I am going to kiss you soon. Love from Caroline.

> From Timothy to Caroline – Remember I kist you and I luve you.

These notes were written in a class where silent, written conversations are the norm, where the teacher writes notes to individual children making demands, and expects the children to write to her regulating *her*. This is a climate that can continue throughout school. It is important if children are to feel they have personal access to their teacher who accepts and enjoys what they write, and, above all, that the reply is personal, in the child's own idiom, and in the context of the topic the *child has initiated*. This is not the place for the teacher to provide a topic. The teacher must not lead but be led in writing by the child.

Teachers may well have to make it clear that they are not always available for individual children to talk to them, and that the only way for children to regulate them is to write notes, but that there will be an opportunity for individual discussion at some point. This is the stuff of which true 'conferencing' is made.

It is the message and the purpose of the message that matters and not the medium – for what shines through all this is the personal concern for each child by a caring teacher.

Writing in school

Teachers long for their children to feel strongly enough about them to be moved to write, for the urgency to come from within.

This urgency will occur in the classroom under these conditions.

- If there have been massive experiences in the world of play as well as in the real world; occasions of exploration and of fun and delight *without* the inevitable 'Now write about it'.
- If there has been sufficient opportunity for children to imitate and identify with other children and adults when they are writing.
- If situations arise where communication cannot be other than on paper.
- Where children have sufficient ease in handwriting and awareness of letter strings that are common and acceptable in their own language for them to write as freely as they speak.

Then children write in school as purposefully and urgently as they do out of school. It is a highly sensitive teacher who can not only enrich and stimulate children, but also train them in handwriting and spelling skills. Fortunately, we do find such teachers who provide in their teaching that subtle blend of enrichment for the message to be worth transmitting, as well as providing such control of the basic skills that the medium will be adequate for the message.

Finally, here are some further examples of written conversations which have taken place in schools, along with a short note from a teacher (Angela Brennan, Cambridge) showing how she started this style of working with the pupils in her class.

Silent conversations

Note from a teacher about silent conversations

When I first started to communicate with these five- and six-year-old children through writing I replied to their pictures and writing by asking them a question about it. As the children got used to this they began to initiate the 'dialogue' more, so that they were no longer simply replying to my questions. The children began to communicate with me, quite spontaneously, through writing. I replied. Silent conversations through writing ensued. As this practice developed in the classroom, the children began to write to each other as well as to me.

PURPOSEFUL WRITING 67

Vikki:
(note brought to school with mum)

Mrs Brennan
I am not well ~~today~~ so
I cannot come to school
Love Vikki

teacher:
(sent this note home to her)

O.K. I have marked you absent on the register.

love from Mrs. Brennan.

Is it tonsilitis?

Vikki
(came with this reply)

no
no it was sore throat

teacher:
What did the doctor do?

Vikki: looked in my cars and she give me some eye drops

ooDxxxD

Stuart:
To christopher I hop you will
Br at School tomohrow

christopher:
Stuart tahk you for the lettr
Why do you want me to come t
sool tommro

Stuart:
because I want to play with you

> Daniel: To Mrs Brennan I hope yuo have a nice time love Danie Jack xxx
>
> teacher: to Daniel, thank you. I hope you have a nice time too.
>   love from Mrs. Brennan. xxx
>
> Daniel: To Mrs Brennan are you stupid Do you think I love you
>
> teacher: yes I do. Do you love me?
>
> Daniel: Fooled you I Do love you
>
> teacher: oh good.
>
> Daniel: Mrs Brennan you are a silly Billy
>
> teacher: I know! Are you silly too?
>
> Daniel: you little rascal But I still love you xx
>
> teacher: And I still love you too.

> James: To andrew I like you
> x x x xx xx x x xxxx x xxxtx x x x x xxx
>
> Andrew: To James I like you
> x t tx xxxxtx x t t

> **Kersti:** To Louise my mum said you are allowed round mine today from Kersti
>
> **Louise:** Yes I will come round yours Louise

> **Louise:**
> mrs Bremnan
> how do you feel today do you feel happy or do you feel sad
> **teacher:** I feel happy. Everyone in here today is lovely and working very hard.
> **Louise:** have you got a hat at home
> **teacher:** yes but I hate wearing it because it squashes my hair. Do you have any hats And do you like them? **Louise:** I have got some hat and I like them

More purposeful writing in school

Teacher:	I like your play and I think we shall be able to act it at the end of term. Can you give Jason more to say? Can you tell me what will happen after the Scouts have rescued him.
Sandy:	Jason does not say much in the cave, but just you wait and see.
Teacher:	OK. Can we talk about this after break this afternoon?

Teacher:	I liked your drawing of a kingfisher. Did you see one on T.V. last night, swooping down after a fish?
Debbie:	Yes I did, and I saw a heron. I liked the kingfisher best.
Teacher:	I haven't ever seen a kingfisher. I have got a bird table. Have you got one?
Debbie:	No, I haven't. My cat got on our one and killed the tits. It was awful, feathers all round and blood.

This is another silent, written conversation between an adult and a six-year-old child.

Adult:	I think you are very clever.
Child:	I think you are very nice.
Adult:	I'm glad because I think you are super.
Child:	Did you like Snow White which dwarf did you like
Adult:	I like Dopey best but I think you prefer Doc
Child:	I like Bashfull best.
Adult:	I liked it when the tortoise bumped down the steps!
Child:	I liked it when Sneezy and Dopey dressed up in the long coat.
Adult:	Wasn't it nice? I had forgotten that one.
Child:	I liked the organ and the bird in a nest.
Adult:	I didn't see the bird in the nest but I did like all the birds sitting round watching her when she was asleep.
Child:	I liked it in the mine with the dimons.

This is writing that is urgent, reciprocal, personal and immediate, and it is one way into the practice of purposeful writing.

References

Hoffman, M., *Reading, Writing and Relevance*, Hodder & Stoughton, London, 1976.

Peters, M. L., *Spelling caught or taught? A new look*, Routledge & Kegan Paul, 1985.

Rosen, H., *Language and Class*, Falling Wall Press, Bristol, 1973.

The neglected 'R'
Christopher Jarman

How to improve handwriting teaching

These days wise teachers do not see a conflict between the value of skill teaching and creativity in writing. From a child's early pre-school years, the encouragement of correct flowing hand movements in writing is not only possible but essential if later competence is to underpin the all-important freedom of expression.

In the Bullock Report (DES, 1975) on language the section on handwriting states:

> The ability to write easily, quickly and legibly affects the *quality* of a child's written output, for difficulty with his handwriting can hamper his thoughts and limit his fluency. If a child is left to develop his handwriting *without instruction* he is unlikely to develop a running hand which is simultaneously legible, fast flowing and individual and becomes effortless to produce. We therefore believe that the teacher should devote time to teaching it and to giving the children ample practice. (11.50)

The guidance given in this chapter is not related to any particular so-called style, but upon the underlying Roman running or cursive hand upon which European writing has been based for 400 years.

Writing is related to patterns and *some* patterns are related to writing. Marion Richardson's error in her handwriting books was in not being selective enough from children's natural patterns in encouraging only those which are suitable for the rather unnatural discipline of the alphabet.

The fundamental pattern of Western European and American handwriting is a series of slightly forward-sloping ovals and straight lines. This has been true from the Anglo-Saxon cursive, and Italian humanist right through to the Victorian copperplate and present day Civil Service styles. That is:

O | O | O | O | O |

Indeed, in the seventeenth century, Edward Cocker, a famous writing master in all styles, wrote his well-known couplet:

On oval wheels should fair Italian run
Smooth as the whirling chariot of the sun.

Ludovigo Arrighi, in Rome, and Roger Ascham, in Cambridge, both took as fundamental this oval and straight line pattern for fast, economical handwriting. This means that certain well-used school patterns are not at all helpful as they do not conform to this rule. They are, for example,

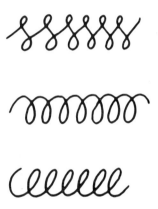

Indeed, in my experience I have found these patterns to be anti-handwriting and actually to make a child's writing worse than before!

For school purposes there are about eight patterns which relate very closely in size and shape to certain good handwriting movements and to some families of well formed letters. These are shown on the next page.

	pattern	related letters
1	mmm	rnmhbpk
2	uuuuu	iltuy
3	ilililili	iltumn
4	ululu	iltuy
5	mmm	nmp
6	wwww	vwx
7	ccccc	coagdqe
8	ooooo	oo oa oc

Of course, once the letter shapes have been learnt, then combination patterns made of letters are also helpful. Especially of groups which would help spelling, for example,

ing ing ing ing ing ing
ion ion ion ion ion ion
ough ough ough ough ough

Teachers should be able to make up many useful word endings and beginnings or common word groups such as:

the the and and

him him as as as

which would make good letter patterns. These patterns could be written around a child's work as an educational border pattern, rather than encouraging mere time-filling processes with oversized wax crayons or spongy felt tips.

The alphabet

The following alphabet is based upon the historic shapes evolved by professional scribes for fast, legible writing. Young children of five years of age are quite capable of learning a joined or cursive hand from the beginning, and in most European countries are taught such a style. Before 1913 infants in all English classes were taught a looped Civil Service hand. Here is an example of a five-year-old writing in such a style today in a primary school.

Five-year-old infant, Wales

The Spring
Spring the sweet Spring
Is the year's pleasant king
Little birds do sing
Wedding bells do ring
Little lambs are prancing
Little birds are singing

This looped style is not shown because it is recommended, only to show that such mature hand control is quite normal at five years old.

Teachers who have been used to teaching print script may prefer to compromise and teach stage one of the basic alphabet. Stages two and three may be reached very rapidly by many individual children. By the age of seven to eight all children ought to be writing a good joined hand. It may be immature in some cases, but such a hand is certainly not beyond the competence of the average top infant.

Stage one: fundamental shapes, based on ovals and straight lines

a b c d e f g h

i j k l m n o p

q r s t u v w

x y z

Notes

1 All letters start at the top except 'e' and 'd'.

2 'f' may have a descender *f* if desired but initially children find the change of direction difficult.

3 'k' is best started as two strokes, as children will often make *R* to begin with.

4 All letters must be made in one flowing movement except 'f', 'k' and 't', which have two.

5 *L* should retain the hook at the base, like the capital 'L'. Then the capital 'I' may be taught economically as one stroke, for example, *I*.

Stage two: adding hooks (or serifs) prior to joining

a b c d e f g

h i j k l m n

o p q r s t u

v w x y z ſ

Notes

1 All letters still start at the top.

2 'f' may be extended.

3 *k* may now be taught in one stroke.

4 The alternative *ſ* is also very useful as it joins more easily.

Stage three: joining where appropriate
Horizontal joins

f o r t

v w x

Diagonal joins

a c d e h i k

l m n u x

No joins necessary

b g j p q s z

Notes

1 *f* and *t* are most quickly and economically joined from their final cross strokes.

for food

ton tin

2 Ascending letters may be linked simply from small letters by a diagonal join if appropriate.

oh ch al

wh il

3 *q* is best left unjoined, as joining from the descender makes an awkward space.

quick queen

as *u* is the most common letter in English to be joined to *q*, the unit *qu* should be practised, with the initial hook of the *u* touching the top of *q*. *qu qu*

4 *bgjps* do not join easily as their finishing strokes move from right to left whereas joining strokes need to move from left to right. It is speedier and more legible therefore to leave them unjoined.

Methods and resources

Very young children need to be shown individually on the paper in front of them how the patterns and letter shapes are made. Little arrows and starting dots may help if their purpose is explained! Many reception class infants cannot copy from the blackboard but as soon as a group is capable of this, it is economical to teach in this way.

Plain paper is best at first, but as soon as children are voluntarily writing their own sentences, lines about 15 mm apart are very suitable. Children will often hang their writing between two lines. This is exactly what the sixteenth century writing masters advised, and it is quite a tidy way of working!

Use all kinds of writing implements. Hard tipped coloured fibre tips are excellent and much better than pencils which have to be sharpened so often.

Why not reward progress in writing by allowing the children to proceed to different colours as they improve?

Good hand control can be encouraged by giving children mazes to follow, as in these examples. They can follow the same maze many times in different colour fibre tips.

Osmiroid Educational, Fareham Road, Gosport, Hants, sell a very good product called LEDA lettershapes. These are grooved plastic boards with good basic shapes arranged in letter families. A pencil or fibre-tip inserted in the groove can only be moved around in the correct direction, due to an ingenious step-down design.

Handwriting must be considered by teachers in exactly the same way as any other physical skill such as netball or football, movement and P.E. or swimming. In other words, teachers must first become both fairly knowledgeable and physically proficient themselves. Then, by arranging regular practice where a particular movement can be analysed and perfected together, a high level of expertise can be achieved by almost all pupils.

Giving out copybooks of patterns and exercises which teachers themselves have not done, and which are only partly understood, is as ineffective as expecting children to learn swimming from reading a book.

The handwriting lesson is a miniature movement lesson. Everything about the learning and teaching of handwriting points to its kinaesthetic nature and the exercise of more and more skilled movements. While the shapes of our Western letters are important, especially in reading, the body's memory of their constructed movements is much more important in writing. To test this, just close your eyes and write the first sentence which comes into your head. You will find that your handwriting, controlled by your body's movements only, is as good as when your eyes are involved. This demonstrates what an enormous percentage of handwriting learning is physical.

With this in mind it is important to consider how to influence our pupils' writing for clarity, legibility and speed. Ten minutes' thoughtless practice per day merely reinforces previous errors. Children on this system seldom improve, and poor hand movements become even more ingrained. On the other hand a carefully planned thirty-minute lesson teaching a particular movement, say, the *coagd* family or the horizontal join *oo vr*, giving the pupils many opportunities to practise those particular movements, can be very effective indeed. Such a lesson twice a week has far more effect than ten minutes' daily practice where only copying is done and no discussion takes place.

Do not forget to share the *Rules of Writing* with the children.

- All letters should start from the top.
- All similar letters should be the same height.
- All down strokes should be parallel to each other.
- All down strokes should be the same distance apart.

Levels of writing

Children need to be helped to understand that there are at least three levels of handwriting. Here they are:

- *Personal and private*
  for note taking, shopping lists, drafting and so on.
- *Public and legible*
  for letter writing, stories, essays, etc.
- *Formal*
  for notice boards, special occasions, job applications, form filling, etc.

It is a great help to young children to be told which level is required for a piece of work. Too often teachers, under the banner of 'standards', expect the inappropriate level 3 handwriting from children at all times. This results in failure for many, and a deliberate limiting of the amount of work possible by the most intelligent children.

Copybooks

Whichever copybooks you choose, try to liaise between reception infant teachers and top junior teachers. Copybooks will never solve your handwriting problems. The teacher must teach writing quite formally, using a page in the copybook as a guide perhaps. Then, as with the use of maths books, they may be given out for the children to revise from the book what they have just learnt. Merely giving out copybooks and hoping that children will improve their own writing from them is a probationer's fantasy!

Examples of children's writing

Here, and on pages 77 and 78 are examples of children's writing with some comments.

This four-year-old was taught (in a kindly way) from the age of about two and a half; first writing his name and then any words he wanted to write. He was always shown small letters before learning capitals, and taught how to start them at the top and make each letter in one movement. Now, at twenty, he has a very pleasant flowing hand.

This six-year-old wrote rather badly until a supply teacher with a keen interest in handwriting took over the class. This letter was written only three weeks later.

Beauty

Today when we to our patch, we had to look for the beaty. I thought that everything was beautiful. I picked away leaf it was a red and a lovely green colour. I bought my back with me. I thought the grave yard looked beautiful. The trees were blom blooming with buds and bright green leaves. I saw bits of grass that were lovely. A few flowers were beautiful. The birds had beautiful colours on them. I saw a catkin in the bog. I got my shoes and socks wet and I got sets scratch on my leg by a bramble. And when we trod in the bog, sometimes we went down a big. The lovely grass I saw in the bog was close by the ivy tree. When we were coming back to school, in the school gardens I saw a tree with pink flowers on and they were beautiful.

This is like the beautiful ivy leaf that I bought back.

by
Bridget Doughty
aged 8

This eight-year-old was printing in her seventh year, but with careful teaching, using patterns and letter families, began to develop a passable hand by the summer term.

June 17th

Perhaps you have seen honeycombs for sale in the dairy-little square wooden frames with a white fitting. The beekeeper puts these wooden frames, empty, into the hive, and the bees build little honey pots of bees wax inside the frames. Then they fill the pots with honey and seal each one with a wax lid. They do this to stop the liquid honey from getting hard and dry, as honey does if we leave it in an open pot.

by Mandy Walker
Age 9

Nine-year-old after changing from a good 'Marion Richardson' joined style as an infant.

Hi handsome hunting man.
Fire your little gun Bang!
Now the animal is dead and dumb and done,
Never more to peep again, creep again, leap again,
Eat or sleep or drink again. Oh, what fun.

Winter at the Doors of Spring.

Wild are the waves
    echoes
    supper
The feather
Jenny wren
The Snowflake
Arithmetic
These Solemn Hills   for Mr Jarman.
  No bed
A Goldfinch

A piece of practice writing by a very artistic ten-year-old boy who had been taught a simple italic style in one year. It was laid on my desk as a small gift!

> **Morse Code**
>
> This morning we had the idea of doing some morse code so we got some second world war ear-phones and a 4½ volt battery. We connected one of the ear-phones wires to one of the battery terminals and took the other terminal's plastic top off. We used the other ear-phones wire to make dots and dashes on the uncovered terminals. A dot was a touch on the top of the screw and a dash was a stroke up the edge of the screw. We copied the morse code out of an encyclopaedia so we could recieve & send messages. Then Mr. Jarman suggested that we used the intercom as that's got a buzzer we could send morse on and we

The first page of a personal project book by an eleven-year-old who had been taught a basic style for about three years. The 'e' joins from the middle are an old tradition but need to be taught carefully to be successful. Joining from the bottom of the 'e' is a perfectly acceptable alternative.

> First it marked out a race course, in a sort of circle, ('the exact shape doesn't matter,' it said,) and then all the party were placed along the course, here and there. There was no 'One, two, three, and away,' but they began running when they liked, so that it was not easy to know when the race was over. However, when they had been running half an hour or so, and were quite dry again, the Dodo suddenly called out 'The race is over!' and they all crowded round it, panting, and asking, 'But who has won?'.

The prize winner in a competition for eleven-year-old preparatory school boys. This is a very well controlled, fast and legible hand which should develop in character throughout adolescence.

Recommended books and schemes

DES, *A Language for Life*, HMSO, 1975.
Jarman, C., *Developing Handwriting Skills*, Blackwell, Oxford, 1979.
Jarman, C., *Handwriting Skills* (6 copybooks), Blackwell, Oxford, 1982.
LEDA Letter formers, Osmiroid Educational, Gosport, Hampshire.
Sassoon, R., *The Practical Guide to Children's Handwriting*, Thames and Hudson, London, 1983.
Barnard, T., *Handwriting Activities Book Two*, Ward Lock Educational, London, 1979.
Fairbank, A., *A Handwriting Manual*, Faber Paperback, London, 1954.
Wellington, I., *The Irene Wellington Copybook*, Canongate, Edinburgh, 1957.

Index

accuracy 55, 56
achievement 14
aesthetic product 32
alphabet 14, 71, 73
anecdotes 33
appreciate 31
appropriateness 27, 49, 50
articulacy 23
attitudes 23, 31
audience 16, 18, 25, 27, 28, 31, 33, 35, 37, 40, 43, 46, 56
author 23, 31, 32, 37
authority 22
authorship 14

bilingualism 48, 51, 52

commitment 20
communicate 17, 55, 66
communicating 15
communication 34, 51, 56, 65, 66
    purposeful 15
communicative act 48
complexity 33, 34
composition 14, 49
conceptual framework 25
confidence 23
content 27, 31, 56
context 15, 16, 20, 23, 38, 43, 49
convention 35
conversation 14, 30, 65
   silent 66
   written 66, 70
correcting 33
correctly 58
correctness 37, 51
correction 45, 49, 50, 51, 58
   self-correction 63
creativity 14, 30, 31, 32, 71
curiosity 17, 25, 40

diagram 44
   flow 45, 46
   tree 44, 45
dialect 48, 49, 50, 51, 52
dialogue 14, 22, 34, 43, 48, 66
differentiation 33

draft 16, 23, 24, 31, 32, 37, 38, 40, 41, 42, 44, 56, 75
   final 42, 43
   re-drafting 31, 32, 43

edit 43
engagement 20
errors, superficial 33
evaluate 17, 31
evaluation 14, 31
experience 20, 22, 23, 24, 25, 26, 27, 32, 33, 52, 53, 66
   aesthetic 31
   daily 37
   first-hand 23, 24, 34, 40
   incidental 13
   personal 13, 22, 23, 40
   previous 25
   productive 20
   sensory 25
   shared 30
   total 31

fantasy 26
form 27, 28, 39

grammar 38
grammatical accuracy 51

haiku 28, 30
handwriting 13, 14, 23, 33, 39, 44, 55, 56, 64, 66, 71, 75, 76

idiom 51
imagination 13, 24
imaginative 37, 38, 50
   effort 37
impersonal 37
inappropriate 65, 75
indentification 20
informative 39
interaction 20

language 23, 26, 27, 28, 31, 50, 51, 66, 71
   development 23
   process 17
   second 50, 51
   spoken 25
   target 51

languages 52, 53
legibility 55, 58, 75
legible 56, 63, 71, 73, 74, 78
legibly 57
letter families 75, 77
    patterns 73
    shapes 75
letters 17, 71, 75, 76
linguistic 56
    conventions 35
    diversity 14, 48, 53
listening 25
logical thought 21

mother tongue 50, 52
motivation 55, 65

narrative 15, 39, 43
    imaginative 38
    personal 34
narrator 35, 37, 38
native speakers 52
non-standard 14, 49, 50
nouns 42

organisation 14, 16, 22, 33, 50

paragraphing 39
personal knowledge 39
    observation 21
    reflections 21, 23
poem 16, 27, 28, 38, 52
poetic 30, 35
poetry 30, 55
pronunciation 51
publish 16, 27, 31
punctuation 39, 45, 49, 50, 55, 58
purpose 15, 16, 17, 20, 21, 22, 23, 26, 27, 46

reality 15
recording 23
reflection 27
response 27
retelling 33

sarcasm 35
self-expression 30
sentence 39, 50, 51, 75

significance 21, 22, 23
society 15, 16
spectator role 25, 35
speech 35, 39, 51, 55, 56
spelling 14, 28, 33, 39, 44, 49, 50, 51, 55, 56, 57, 63, 64, 65, 66, 72
spontaneity 24, 65, 66
structure 39, 43, 44, 46
    awareness of 33
    informative 40
    sentence 23, 40, 45
    underlying 33, 39
standard 14, 48, 49, 50, 53
structures 14, 34, 38
style 21, 34, 39, 42, 58, 64, 66, 73, 77, 78
    formal 42
    informative 42
    impersonal 42
    literary 42
subordination 50
surface features 33, 46
syntax 35, 56, 57, 64, 65

transactional 37, 39

urgency 55, 56

verbs 39
vocabulary 23, 30
voice 13, 14, 16, 17, 22, 23, 28, 30

word groups 73
words 76
writers, real 17, 19
    fluent 42, 50
writing, creative 28, 31, 62
    development 13, 33
    expressive 25
    personal 25, 28, 31
    procedure 17
    process of 14, 15, 16, 20, 48
    purposeful 14, 20, 55, 56, 57, 63, 65, 70
    real 13, 16, 17
    relevant 56
    types of 14
    urgent 56, 65
written medium 44
    conversations 66, 70

Help with homework

French revision

"HI, MY NAME IS KITCAT..."

"... AND I'M DIG"

"WE ARE HERE TO HELP YOU LEARN FRENCH. START AT THE BEGINNING AND DON'T DO TOO MUCH IN ONE GO."

"STICK WITH IT (EVEN WHEN THE GRAMMAR GETS TO YOU), LEARN THE KEY VOCABULARY AND YOU'LL SOON BE SPEAKING LE FRANÇAIS!! SEE YOU LATER – À PLUS TARD!"

Written by Nina Filipek
Designed and illustrated by Dan Green

Autumn Publishing

www.autumnchildrensbooks.co.uk

how do you say...?

Learn how to say the sounds of the letters. If you don't know how to say a word you can follow the pronunciation guide set within the brackets.

stick a reward sticker here!

vowels

a (as in b**a**t) for **salon** (salohn)

à (as in **a**nt) for **là** (la)

â (as in p**a**sta) for **pâtes** (paht)

é (as in caf**e**) for **marché** (marshay)

è (as in **e**gg) for **père** (pear)

i (as in f**i**eld) for **il** (eel)

î (as in feel) for **île** (eeluh)

o (as in g**o**t) for **bon** (bohn)

ô (as in **o**val) for **hôtel** (ohtel)

œ (as 'ir' in b**ir**d) for **sœur** (sir)

u (as in r**u**de) for **rue** (roo)

ù (as in t**u**be) for **où** (ooh)

nasal sounds

These nasal sounds are pronounced 'through the nose'. Look out for them when a vowel appears before an 'n'.

ans (ahn)

médecin (maydesan)

bon (bohn)

un (un)

chien (sheyan)

consonants

French consonants are pronounced more clearly than English consonants, e.g. the 'r' is 'rolled' at the back of the mouth. However, there are some exceptions: 'h' is never pronounced.

homme (om)

hôtel (ohtel)

JE SUIS UN CHIEN.
I AM A DOG.

syllables

In English, we tend to stress the first part of a word and then slur the remaining syllables, whereas in French, the syllables are equally stressed. Try it:

professeur (pro-fess-ur)

conversation (con-ver-sas-iyon)

médecin (may-de-san)

male and female nouns

In French, nouns (i.e. people, places and things) are either masculine (**un** or **le**) or feminine (**une** or **la**).

For example:

Masculine
un chien – a dog
le chien – the dog

A French dictionary will tell you whether a noun is masculine or feminine.

Feminine
une maison – a house
la maison – the house

plurals

Add **'s'** to the noun unless it ends in **s**, **x** or **z** in which case there is no change.

Add **'x'** when the noun ends in **eau** and **eu**.

For example:
un fils, les fils – son, sons
un gâteau, les gâteaux – cake, cakes

l'alphabet
the alphabet

Learning to say the alphabet in French is useful for times when you are asked to spell something, for example, your name.

A	ah	**H**	ash	**O**	oh	**V**	vay
B	bay	**I**	ee	**P**	pay	**W**	double-vay
C	say	**J**	juh	**Q**	koo	**X**	eex
D	day	**K**	ka	**R**	air	**Y**	ee grek
E	ugh	**L**	el	**S**	es	**Z**	zed
F	ef	**M**	em	**T**	tay		
G	zjay	**N**	en	**U**	oo		

Spell these names aloud in French.

For example: C-L-A-R-A would be spelled: say-el-ah-air-ah.

P-I-E-R-R-E

A-N-T-O-I-N-E

P-A-S-C-A-L

S-A-B-I-N-E

L-A-U-R-E

C-O-L-E-T-T-E

NOW SPELL ALOUD YOUR NAME IN FRENCH.

Can you work out what these place names are?

1. pay-ah-air-ee-es _____

2. el-ee grek-oh-en _____

3. en-ee-say-ugh _____

4. bay-oh-air-day-ugh-ah-oo-eex _____

5. zjay-air-ugh-en-oh-bay-el-ugh _____

6. say-ah-el-ah-ee-es _____

Now write the place names in the correct places on this map of France.

6. _____

1. _____

FRANCE

2. _____

5. _____

4. _____

3. _____

ESPAGNE

stick a reward sticker here!

Can you add any other place names to the map, e.g. Toulouse?

salut!
hello!

Revise these basic French words and phrases.

Oui – Yes
Non – No
Salut! – Hi
Bonjour – Hello
Bonne nuit – Goodnight
Au revoir – Goodbye
À bientôt – See you soon
S'il vous plaît – Please
Merci – Thank you
Excusez-moi / Pardon – Sorry

BONJOUR

Draw lines to join the answers to the questions in the conversation below.

ÇA VA?
HOW ARE YOU?

J'AI DIX ANS.
I AM 10 YEARS OLD.

COMMENT T'APPELLES-TU?
WHAT IS YOUR NAME?

J'HABITE A' LONDRES.
I LIVE IN LONDON.

QUEL AGE AS-TU?
HOW OLD ARE YOU?

TRÈS BIEN, MERCI. ET TOI?
VERY WELL, THANK YOU. AND YOU?

OU HABITES-TU?
WHERE DO YOU LIVE?

JE M'APPELLE MICHEL.
MY NAME IS MICHEL.

remember: in French we use 'vous' when talking to people we don't know and 'tu' when talking among friends.

stick a reward sticker here!

Now answer these questions about yourself. Write the answers in French inside the speech bubbles.

ÇA VA?

COMMENT T'APPELLES-TU?

QUÊL AGE AS-TU?

OU HABITES-TU?

stick a reward sticker here!

nombres
numbers

stick a reward sticker here!

Revise the words for the numbers in French before you move on to the activities below!

0	zéro	11	onze	21	vingt et un	40	quarante
1	un / une	12	douze	22	vingt-deux	50	cinquante
2	deux	13	treize	23	vingt-trois	60	soixante
3	trois	14	quatorze	24	vingt-quatre	70	soixante-dix
4	quatre	15	quinze	25	vingt-cinq	71	soixante-onze
5	cinq	16	seize	26	vingt-six	80	quatre-vingts
6	six	17	dix-sept	27	vingt-sept	90	quatre-vingt-dix
7	sept	18	dix-huit	28	vingt-huit	100	cent
8	huit	19	dix-neuf	29	vingt-neuf	101	cent un
9	neuf	20	vingt	30	trente	200	deux cents
10	dix			31	trente et un…	201	deux cent un

How many are there? Write the answers in French.

_____ bananes

_____ carottes

_____ œufs

_____ raisins

How much do they weigh? Write the answers in French.

_____ grammes

_____ grammes

_____ grammes

_____ grammes

Read the prices in French, then write the numbers in the price tags:

remember: French currency is euros.

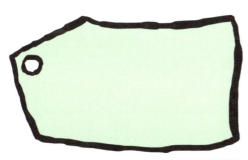

vingt et un euros

soixante-sept euros

cinquante euros

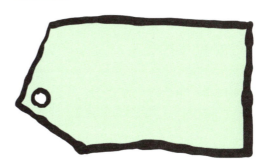

quatre-vingt-dix-neuf euros

les mois de l'année
the months of the year

remember: in French, months and days don't start with a capital letter unless they are at the beginning of a sentence.

Revise the months of the year in French:

janvier – January
février – February
mars – March
avril – April
mai – May
juin – June
juillet – July
août – August
septembre – September
octobre – October
novembre – November
décembre – December

Draw lines to match the French to the English translations.

le vingt-cinq décembre	le trente et un octobre
2nd April	le premier janvier
31st October	18th March
1st January	12th July
le douze juillet	25th December
le dix-huit mars	le deux avril

quelle est la date de ton anniversaire? When is your birthday?

Write the answer on the lines below in French and English.

Mon anniversaire est le _____.

My birthday is the _____ .

Translate the birthdays into English and write them in the diary.

"LE VINGT FÉVRIER"

"LE DIX AOÛT"

"LE VINGT-SIX MAI"

stick a reward sticker here!

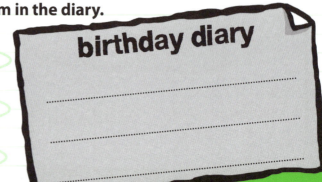

birthday diary

les jours de la semaine
the days of the week

stick a reward sticker here!

Revise the days of the week in French:

lundi – Monday **jeudi** – Thursday **dimanche** – Sunday
mardi – Tuesday **vendredi** – Friday
mercredi – Wednesday **samedi** – Saturday

Write these dates in French.

Tuesday 5th November   *mardi cinq novembre*

Saturday 23rd September   _____

Wednesday 17th June   _____

Sunday 4th December   _____

What is your favourite day of the week?   _____

What is the day and date today?   _____

festivals – festivals

Here are some festival dates for your diary.

Veille de Noël – Christmas Eve, 24th December
Jour de Noël – Christmas Day, 25th December
Saint-Sylvestre – New Year's Eve, 31st December
Jour de l'An – New Year's Day, 1st January
Épiphanie – Epiphany, 6th January
14 juillet or **Fête Nationale** – Bastille Day, 14th July

quelle heure est-il?
what time is it?

stick a reward sticker here!

Say aloud the times in French on the clocks below.

Il est une heure.

Il est six heures.

Il est huit heures et quart.

Il est trois heures et demie.

Il est dix heures moins le quart.

Draw the hands on the clocks to show these times.

Il est dix heures.

Il est quatre heures et demie.

Il est neuf heures moins le quart.

Il est six heures et quart.

remember: demi has an 'e' (demie) when it comes after the hours because hour is a feminine noun.

horaire de bus – bus timetable

To…	Departure times
Paris	5:00
Lyon	11:45
Calais	2:15
Marseille	7:30
Bordeaux	1:00
Toulouse	9:30

Read the bus timetable and answer the questions in French.

for example:

À quelle heure est le bus à Paris?   *À cinq heures.*
At what time is the bus to Paris?

1. À quelle heure est le bus à Lyon? _____
2. À quelle heure est le bus à Calais? _____
3. À quelle heure est le bus à Marseille? _____
4. À quelle heure est le bus à Bordeaux? _____
5. À quelle heure est le bus à Toulouse? _____

Answer these questions in French about your daily routine.

What time did you get up this morning? _____

What time does school start? _____

What time do you eat lunch? _____

What time do you go to bed? _____

stick a reward sticker here!

les vêtements
clothes

stick a reward sticker here!

Revise the French words for these items of clothing:

- **un tee-shirt** – a T-shirt
- **un chemisier** – a blouse
- **une jupe** – a skirt
- **un jean** – jeans
- **un short** – shorts
- **une robe** – a dress
- **une veste** – a jacket
- **les chaussures** – shoes
- **les lunettes de soleil** – sunglasses
- **un chapeau** – a hat
- **les chaussettes** – socks
- **un cardigan** – a cardigan
- **un jogging** – a tracksuit

See if you can find 10 items of clothing in this word search. Look across and down the grid.

g	v	r	v	b	h	s	b	t	l	c
x	c	h	e	m	i	s	i	e	r	h
t	h	k	s	l	j	m	i	e	o	a
a	a	k	t	q	o	c	p	s	b	p
q	u	u	e	p	g	p	b	h	e	e
h	s	m	l	b	g	l	d	i	e	a
v	s	n	j	p	i	r	p	r	p	u
j	u	p	e	x	n	w	t	t	d	t
w	r	e	a	a	g	l	d	l	s	e
e	e	p	n	t	r	i	c	o	t	a
z	s	x	c	a	r	d	i	g	a	n

14

les animaux
animals

stick a reward sticker here!

Learn the French words for these pets:

un chien – a dog
un chat – a cat
un poisson rouge – a gold fish
un oiseau – a bird
un cheval – a horse
un lapin – a rabbit
un hamster – a hamster
une souris – a mouse
une tortue – a tortoise

avez-vous un animal domestique?
Do you have a pet?

J'AI...
I HAVE...

JE N'AI PAS D'ANIMAUX.
I HAVEN'T GOT ANY PETS.

Match the owners to their pets.

1
J'AI UN CHEVAL.

2
J'AI UNE TORTUE ET DEUX SOURIS.

3
J'AI TROIS CHATS.

4
J'AI DEUX LAPINS.

a, b, c, d

AVEZ-VOUS UN ANIMAL DOMESTIQUE?
DO YOU HAVE A PET?

couleurs
colours

Some colours can be either masculine or feminine to match the nouns they describe. The 'e' ending matches feminine nouns **(f)**:

vert / verte – green
bleu / bleue – blue
gris / grise – grey
noir / noire – black
blanc / blanche – white
violet / violette – purple

for example:

une fleur **(f)** bleue
(a blue flower)

un lapin **(m)** gris
(a grey rabbit)

Some colours can be used with both masculine and feminine nouns and the ending does not need to change:

orange – orange
marron – brown
rose – pink

rouge – red
jaune – yellow
argent – silver

or – gold

Draw lines to translate these phrases from English to French:

the brown dog	le chapeau rouge
the red hat	le tee-shirt bleu
two white rabbits	le chien marron
the blue T-shirt	deux lapins blancs

remember:
you need to match the colour ending to the masculine or feminine nouns they describe!

Colour these pictures in the correct colours:

les chaussettes orange

une montre en or

deux chats noirs

une fleur violette

une jupe rouge

un cheval gris

stick a reward sticker here!

moi!
me!

stick a reward sticker here!

When describing yourself you will need two important verbs. Remember the verb endings let you know who is being talked about in the sentence!

AVOIR	J'AI	ÊTRE	JE SUIS
TO HAVE	I HAVE	TO BE	I AM

tu peux te décrire?
Can you describe yourself?

J'AI... / I HAVE...

- **les cheveux blonds** – blonde hair
- **les cheveux bruns** – brown hair
- **les cheveux noirs** – black hair
- **les cheveux roux** – red hair
- **les cheveux longs** – long hair
- **les cheveux courts** – short hair
- **les cheveux ondulés** – wavy hair
- **les cheveux raides** – straight hair
- **les cheveux frisés** – curly hair
- **les yeux verts** – green eyes
- **les yeux bleus** – blue eyes
- **les yeux marron** – brown eyes

JE SUIS... / I AM...

- **grand/e** – tall
- **petit/e** – short
- **mince** – slim
- **gros/grosse** – fat
- **très** – very

remember: 'hair' is a masculine plural noun so we use masculine plural adjectives, with the exception of 'marron' which does not have a plural.

remember: the endings are masculine or feminine depending on the gender of the person we are talking about.

for example:
A boy would say, 'Je suis grand.' I am tall.
A girl would say, 'Je suis grande.' I am tall.

Match the correct description to each of the cats.

remember:
Cheveux = hair for people
Poils = hair for animals

a

b

c

1. Je suis grand et mince. J'ai les poils courts.

2. J'ai les poils longs et frisés. Je suis petite.

3. Je suis très petit et gros.

Colour the cats to match their descriptions.

1. J'ai les yeux verts et les poils blonds.

2. J'ai les poils roux et les yeux marron.

3. J'ai les poils bruns et les yeux bleus.

Now write a sentence in French to describe what you look like.

_____

_____

stick a reward sticker here!

ma famille
my family

Revise the French words for members of the family:

mère – mother
père – father
fille – daughter
fils – son
sœur – sister
frère – brother
grand-mère – grandmother
grand-père – grandfather

Practise talking about your family using the questions and answers below.

Tu as un frère ou une sœur?
Do you have a brother or a sister?

Oui, j'ai un frère et une sœur.
Yes, I have a brother and a sister.

Ma sœur s'appelle Lola.
My sister is called Lola.

Oui, j'ai deux sœurs.
Yes, I have two sisters.

Elle a six ans.
She is six years old.

Non, je suis fils/fille unique.
No, I am an only (m/f) child.

Il y a combien de personnes dans ta famille?
How many people are there in your family?

Il y a quatre personnes dans ma famille: ma mère, mon père, mon frère et moi.
There are four people in my family: my mother, my father, my brother and me.

stick a reward sticker here!

Using Michel's description of his family, fill in the missing names under their pictures and colour in the correct hair and eye colour.

JE M'APPELLE MICHEL. J'AI LES CHEVEUX ROUX ET LES YEUX VERTS.

J'AI UN FRÈRE. MON FRÈRE S'APPELLE MARCEL. MARCEL A LES CHEVEUX NOIRS ET LES YEUX VERTS.

MA MÈRE S'APPELLE JULIETTE. ELLE A LES CHEVEUX BRUNS ET LES YEUX BLEUS.

MON PÈRE S'APPELLE PIERRE. IL A LES CHEVEUX NOIRS ET LES YEUX MARRON.

_____   _____   _____   _____

Look at the family tree. Pretend you are Nicole. Complete the sentences below using the following words:

Louis   deux   sept
Isabelle   six
quarante-sept   un

1. J'ai _____ sœurs.

2. Ma mère s'appelle _____.

3. J'ai _____ frère.

4. Mon père a _____ ans.

5. Mon frère s'appelle _____.

6. Lucie a _____ ans.

7. Il y a _____ personnes dans ma famille.

mes loisirs
my free time

stick a reward sticker here!

Le sport – sports

le football – football
le cricket – cricket
la gymnastique – gymnastics
le ski – skiing
la natation – swimming
l'équitation – horse riding

le vélo – cycling
la danse – dancing
le tennis – tennis
le judo – judo
le basket-ball – basketball

Which of the French words matches each picture? Circle the answer in each line.

1.    la danse   la natation   le vélo

2.   le football   le ski   la gymnastique

3.    le cricket   l'équitation   la danse

4.    la danse   le tennis   l'équitation

5.    le tennis   le cricket   le judo

Quel est votre sport préféré?
_____
What is your favourite sport?

JOUER À /AU – to play *(sport)*
Jouer au tennis – to play tennis
Jouer au football – to play football

JOUER DE/DU – to play *(musical instrument)*

Jouer de la guitare – to play the guitar
Jouer du piano – to play the piano

ALLER À LA/AU – to go

Aller au cinéma – to go to the cinema
Aller à la plage – to go to the beach

J'AIME... I LIKE...

JE N'AIME PAS... I DON'T LIKE...

J'AIME BEAUCOUP... I LIKE A LOT...

for example:
J'aime la gymnastique. I like gymnastics.
Je n'aime pas jouer au cricket. I do not like to play cricket.

Draw lines to match these sentences to the likes and dislikes shown in the pictures.

a

1. J'aime la natation.

b

2. Je n'aime pas jouer au tennis.

c

3. J'aime beaucoup aller au cinéma.

d

4. Je n'aime pas jouer de la guitare.

5. J'aime jouer au football.

e

6. J'aime beaucoup jouer au basket-ball.

f

Write a few sentences about what you like and dislike.

_____

_____

stick a reward sticker here!

le temps
the weather

stick a reward sticker here!

quel temps fait-il? What is the weather like?

il fait beau – it is fine
il fait chaud – it is hot
il fait froid – it is cold
il fait beau temps – it is good weather
il fait mauvais temps – it is bad weather
il fait soleil – it is sunny

il y a du vent – it is windy
il pleut – it is raining
il neige – it is snowing
le ciel est couvert – it is cloudy
il y a de l'orage – there is a storm

Draw lines to match the words to the pictures.

a

b

Il fait soleil

Il neige

c

d

le ciel est couvert

Il y a du vent

Il fait chaud

e

f

Il fait froid

Les saisons de l'année – the seasons of the year

au printemps – in spring
en été – in summer
en automne – in autumn
en hiver – in winter

Are these statements true (vrai) or false (faux)? Look at each picture then circle the correct answer.

1. En hiver il fait chaud.

Vrai or **Faux**

2. Au printemps il pleut.

Vrai or **Faux**

3. En été il fait froid et il neige.

Vrai or **Faux**

4. En automne il y a du vent.

Vrai or **Faux**

Describe what the weather is like now.

_____

_____

stick a reward sticker here!

au marché
at the market

stick a reward sticker here!

VOUS DÉSIREZ?
WHAT WOULD YOU LIKE?

JE VOUDRAIS...
I WOULD LIKE...

une baguette – a stick of bread
des tomates – some tomatoes
des poires – some pears
des oranges – some oranges
des pommes – some apples
des choux – some cabbages
du fromage – some cheese

un oignon – an onion
un citron – a lemon
des carottes – some carrots
des fraises – some strawberries
des œufs – some eggs
du saumon – some salmon
une saucisse – a sausage

remember:
there are two words for 'a' in French.

Un for a masculine noun, e.g. Je voudrais un gâteau.
– I want a cake.

Une for a feminine noun, e.g. Je voudrais une baguette.
– I want a stick of bread.

If we want more than one thing, we say the number of how many we want and make the noun plural.

Complete the following sentences with these words:

un   cinq   deux   une

Je voudrais _____ citron.

Je voudrais _____ pommes.

Je voudrais _____ baguette.

Je voudrais _____ tomates.

stick a reward sticker here!

le restaurant
the restaurant

stick a reward sticker here!

Read the dialogue between the customer and the waiter.

Le menu, s'il vous plaît.
THE MENU, PLEASE.

Merci.
THANK YOU.

Que voulez-vous manger?
WHAT WOULD YOU LIKE TO EAT?

Que voulez-vous boire?
WHAT WOULD YOU LIKE TO DRINK?

Le menu – the menu

Using the picture clues, choose nine words from the list below to fill in the crossword.

ASPERGES – ASPARAGUS
BIFTECK – STEAK
CHAMPIGNONS – MUSHROOMS
CHOUFLEUR – CAULIFLOWER
CRÈME GLACÉE – ICE CREAM
CRÊPE – PANCAKE
FRAISES – STRAWBERRIES
FRITES – CHIPS
FROMAGE – CHEESE
HARICOTS VERTS – GREEN BEANS
LÉGUMES – VEGETABLES
OMELETTE – OMELETTE
PETITS POIS – PEAS
PIZZA – PIZZA
POISSON – FISH
POTAGE – SOUP
POULET – CHICKEN
SAUCISSE – SAUSAGE

Bon appétit!
ENJOY YOUR MEAL.

Match the order to the picture.

1. Je voudrais une omelette et des frites.
2. Je voudrais une bouteille d'eau et une pizza.
3. Je voudrais une soupe et un café.
4. Je voudrais un sandwich au jambon.
5. Je voudrais une salade et une limonade.

a
b
c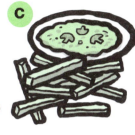
d
e

Read through the conversation between the waiter and customer:

- VOUS DÉSIREZ?
- POUR COMMENCER, JE VOUDRAIS UNE SOUPE À L'OIGNON, S'IL VOUS PLAÎT.
- ET LE PLAT PRINCIPAL?
- JE VOUDRAIS UN BIFTECK ET DES FRITES, S'IL VOUS PLAÎT.
- ÇA SERA TOUT?
- ET UNE SALADE.
- ET COMME BOISSON?
- UN JUS D'ORANGE, S'IL VOUS PLAÎT.
- ET EN DESSERT?
- UNE CRÉME GLACÉE A LA FRAISE, S'IL VOUS PLAIT.
- MERCI, MADAME.

remember:
'J'aime' is 'I like' and 'Je n'aime pas' is 'I do not like'.

J'aime...   Je n'aime pas...

nourriture épicée – spicy food

cuisine française – French food

cuisine italienne – Italian food

cuisine chinoise – Chinese food

nourriture végétarienne – vegetarian food

dans la ville
in the town

où est…? Where is…?

la banque – the bank

le parc – the park

le musée – the museum

le cinéma – the cinema

la gare routière – the bus station

l'école – the school

la pharmacie – the pharmacy

stick a reward sticker here!

Un plan de ville – a town map

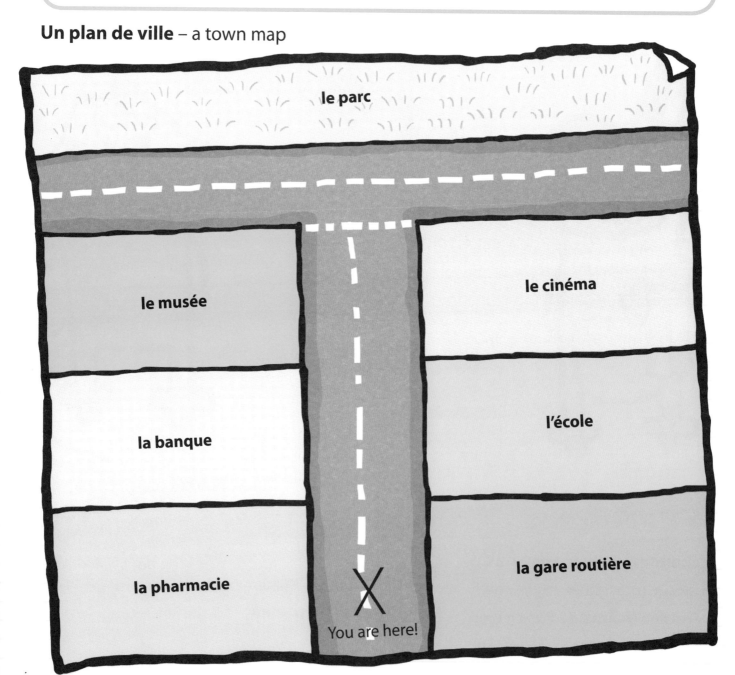

Directions – directions

allez tout droit – go straight ahead

c'est à gauche – it's on the left

c'est à droite – it's on the right

c'est à côté du/de la – it's next to

remember: we use du (masculine), de la (feminine) and de l' (before a vowel).

Read the map on the opposite page and write the answers to the questions below. The first one has been done for you.

1. Où est la banque? *C'est à gauche, à côté de la pharmacie*

2. Où est l'école? _____

3. Où est le parc? _____

4. Où est le musée? _____

5. Où est le cinéma? _____

6. Où est la pharmacie? _____

7. Où est la gare routière? _____

Transport – transport

Learn these useful French words for different types of transport.

le train – the train

le métro – the underground

l'autobus or **le bus** – the bus

la moto – the motorbike

la voiture – the car

l'avion – the airplane

le bac or **le ferry** – the ferry

le taxi – the taxi

stick a reward sticker here!

answers

pages 4-5
1. Paris
2. Lyon
3. Nice
4. Bordeaux
5. Grenoble
6. Calais

page 6-7
Ça va? – Très bien, merci. Et toi?
Comment t'appelles-tu?
– Je m'appelle Michel.
Quel âge as-tu? – J'ai dix ans.
Où habites-tu? – J'habite à Londres.

pages 8-9
sept bananes
douze carottes
seize œufs
vingt et un raisins

100g – cent grammes
78g – soixante-dix-huit grammes
135g – cent trente-cinq grammes
205g – deux cent cinq grammes

vingt et un euros – **21**
soixante-sept euros – **67**
cinquante euros – **50**
quatre-vingt-dix-neuf euros – **99**

pages 10-11
le vingt-cinq décembre – 25th December
2nd April – le deux avril
31st October – le trente et un octobre
1st January – le premier janvier
le douze juillet – 12th July
le dix-huit mars – 18th March

le vingt février – 20th February
le dix août – 10th August
le vingt-six mai – 26th May

Saturday 23rd September – samedi vingt-trois septembre
Wednesday 17th June – mercredi dix-sept juin
Sunday 4th December – dimanche quatre décembre

pages 12-13
Il est dix heures. **(10:00)**
Il est neuf heures moins le quart. **(8:45)**
Il est quatre heures et demie. **(4:30)**
Il est six heures et quart. **(6:15)**

1. À onze heures quarante-cinq / midi moins le quart. .
2. À deux heures et quart.
3. À sept heures et demie.
4. À une heure.
5. À neuf heures et demie.

pages 14-15

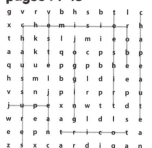

1 – c
2 – d
3 – b
4 – a

pages 16-17
the brown dog – le chien marron
the red hat – le chapeau rouge
two white rabbits – deux lapins blancs
the blue T-shirt – le tee-shirt bleu

les chaussettes orange – **orange socks**
un montre en or – **a gold watch**
deux chats noirs – **two black cats**
une fleur violette – **a purple flower**
une jupe rouge – **a red skirt**
un cheval gris – **a grey horse**

pages 18-19
Je suis grand et mince. J'ai les poils courts.
I am tall and thin. I have short hair. *(male)* **1c**
J'ai les poils longs et frisés. Je suis petite.
I have long curly hair. I am short. *(female)* **2a**
Je suis très petit et gros.
I am very short and fat. *(male)* **3b**

1. J'ai les yeux verts et les poils blonds. *Green eyes, blonde hair*
2. J'ai les poils roux et les yeux marron. *Red hair, brown eyes*
3. J'ai les poils bruns et les yeux bleus. *Brown hair, blue eyes*

pages 20-21
1. J'ai deux sœurs.
2. Ma mère s'appelle Isabelle.
3. J'ai un frère.
4. Mon père a quarante-sept ans.
5. Mon frère s'appelle Louis.
6. Lucie a sept ans.
7. Il y a six personnes dans ma famille.

pages 22-23
1. la natation
2. le football
3. la danse
4. l'équitation
5. le tennis

1. J'aime la natation – **e**
2. Je n'aime pas jouer au tennis – **b**
3. J'aime beaucoup aller au cinéma – **c**
4. Je n'aime pas jouer de la guitare – **f**
5. J'aime jouer au football – **a**
6. J'aime beaucoup jouer au basket-ball – **d**

pages 24-25
Il fait soleil – **d**
Il neige – **f**
Le ciel est couvert – **e**
Il y a du vent – **a**
Il fait chaud – **c**
Il fait froid – **b**

1. En hiver il fait chaud. *(Faux – False)*
2. Au printemps il pleut. *(Vrai – True)*
3. En été il fait froid et il neige. *(Faux – False)*
4. En automne il y a du vent. *(Vrai – True)*

pages 26-27
Je voudrais **un** citron.
Je voudrais **deux** pommes.
Je voudrais **une** baguette.
Je voudrais **cinq** tomates.

pages 28-29

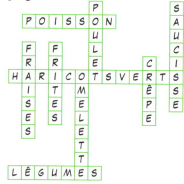

1. Je voudrais une omelette et des frites – **c**
2. Je voudrais une bouteille d'eau et une pizza – **a**
3. Je voudrais une soupe et un café – **d**
4. Je voudrais un sandwich au jambon – **e**
5. Je voudrais une salade et une limonade – **b**

pages 30-31
Possible answers
1. C'est à gauche, à côté de la pharmacie.
2. C'est à droite, à côté du cinéma et de la gard routiere.
3. Allez tout droit.
4. C'est à gauche, à côté de la banque.
5. C'est à droite, à côté de l'école.
6. C'est à gauche, à côté de la banque.
7. C'est à droite, à côté de l'école.